THE QUESTIONS ARE UNDENIABLE.

- How much did the government know about the A-bomb before targeting Japan?
- What do the mysterious symbols on the dollar bill stand for?
- What was kept from the public during the Iran-Contra affair?
- What should we know about the Philadelphia Experiment?

THE ANSWERS ARE UNBELIEVABLE.

Conspiracies and Cover-ups

The one book that dares to
question everything *they h...........* us.

CONSPIRACIES
and COVER-UPS

DAVID ALEXANDER

BERKLEY BOOKS, NEW YORK

CONSPIRACIES AND COVER-UPS

A Berkley Book / published by arrangement with
the author

PRINTING HISTORY
Berkley edition / May 2002

Copyright © 2002 by David Alexander
Book design by Julie Rogers
Cover design by Pyrographx
Cover photographs by AP/Wide World Photos

Visit our website at
www.penguinputnam.com

ISBN: 0-425-18383-1

BERKLEY®
Berkley Books are published by The Berkley Publishing Group,
a division of Penguin Putnam Inc., 375 Hudson Street,
New York, New York 10014.
BERKLEY and the "B" design
are trademarks belonging to Penguin Putnam Inc.

PRINTED IN THE UNITED STATES OF AMERICA

10 9 8 7 6 5 4 3 2

Between the acting of a dreadful thing
And the first motion, all the interim is
Like a phantasma, or a hideous dream:
The Genius and the mortal instruments
Are then in council; and the state of man,
Like to a little kingdom, suffers then
The nature of an insurrection.

WILLIAM SHAKESPEARE
Julius Caesar, Act II, Scene I

CONTENTS ⬛

The End: An Introduction to the Apocalypse

The French have a word for it—*fin de siècle*, the end of the century. It's a time marked by strangeness and uncertainty, fertile ground in which conspiracy theories can take root.

In our time, the world is entering a new millennium as well as a new century, and millennial periods are often believed to be "end times" where apocalyptic developments lie just around the corner.

The American mind-set is especially prone to the influence of doomsday prophesy. Almost 50 percent of Americans believe that the end of history is foretold in the Bible, according to recent polls. Right from the start the Pilgrims, believing they were founding a New Jerusalem, implanted the apocalyptic beliefs of Old

World evangelical movements from the cultural womb of Europe to the embryonic American colonies.

It's not so surprising, then, that in this fin de siècle period we've quantum-shifted from the merely strange to the hyperstrange and that conspiracy theorizing has warped into overdrive.

From Monicagate to embargoed Iraqi weapons programs, factoids compete for media bandwidth. The air seems charged with a bad electricity, crackling with the hot blue ozone of imminent doom. Dark forces lurk hidden behind apparently commonplace events, secretly directing their courses for sinister reasons known only to a furtive cabal of villainous schemers.

The righteous voice of authority is challenged, even mocked, when it offers official explanations for events of all description. The most dire catastrophes and the most innocuous nonevents alike seem linked in outlandish ways when hidden connections are disclosed.

Little can be believed and nothing can be taken at face value. It seems like virtually anything conceivable is possible, that anything can happen—and sometimes it even does.

Nothing is what it seems to be. Beneath the surface lurk untold evils, and beneath these, still graver evils as numerous as angels dancing on the head of a pin. And when the rare bona fide news story breaks that is actually and incontrovertibly incredible, it's like nuclear fuel thrown into a chain reaction, raising the level of conspiracy hysteria another notch closer to critical mass.

These are precarious times in which to live. It's obvious to all that the world is on the brink of something, maybe even apocalypse, yet one person's idea of what lies just over the cusp, into the dawn of this new century, is no better and no worse than anyone else's.

Will it be the angelic choirs of the New Jerusalem or the locust swarms of the Bottomless Pit that greet us as the new millennium unfolds? The so-called experts really haven't a clue, and the credibility of expertise itself has been cast into question by the track records of the intellectual and political aristocracy over the last hundred years.

Yesterday's thinkmeisters failed to predict World War I and were certain it would be over in a few months once it finally began. They failed to squash Hitler when he was still a baby cockroach and thus paved the way for World War II. They failed to roll back Stalin from Eastern Europe and Mao from China, thus paving the way for Vietnam and the cold war. They lied to us about the missile gap, nuclear radiation experiments, the sex lives of our presidents and even the fifty-cent subway fare.

So it's not very surprising that confidence in the credibility of authority is at an all-time low and trust in the motives of society's leaders seems as anachronistic as a spiked helmet on the head of a Hun.

Once the leaders of society lose their credibility, as ours have done, in a procession of fallen figures from Richard Nixon to Newt Gingrich to Bill Clinton, new truthsayers arise to challenge them with alternative models of reality that are better attuned to the belief systems of the populace.

This has happened today as conspiracy theorists emerge from every crack in the wall like the prophets of the old Testament from caves in the Sinai, crying out warnings of strange portents and terrible omens, demanding repentance as the only sure road to salvation. They don't call them "prophets of doom" for nothing, folks. The prophets of old were the ancient equivalents of contemporary conspiracy theorists, and for as long as there have been prophets, they have preached of dire things to come, rarely of good, unless the reward of heaven is preceded by the cleansing fires of a season in hell.

At another time and place in history, in the middle decades of the eighteenth century, another class of truthsayers, the *philosophes* (pronounced fill-eh-zofs), arose in the streets and drawing rooms of Paris to denounce what they called *l'infame*—the "Infamy" of the ruling class.

A few years later, once their radical theories had taken root in the minds of their countrymen, came the French Revolution with the tumbrils clattering through the cobbled streets leading toward the guillotine in the Place de la Concorde that crushed the Infamy but substituted another and worse atrocity in its stead.

Ideas do indeed have consequences, especially when enough people believe in them and volatile circumstances create a powder keg situation waiting for a match to ignite it. Conspiracy, whether real or imagined, or even a mixture of both, has often been midwife to violent revolution. It pays to be very careful about who you listen to and even more careful about the lead-

4

ers you follow, because conspiracy theory is a lit fuse.

The truthsayers, the wannabe leaders, tend to use conspiracy theory as a kind of information freebie, a mind-blowing giveaway that acts almost like a hallucinatory drug. It can hook the mind, and they know it well. The truthsayer's line is that his word is law. Only he and his followers hold the key to the future.

Throughout the literature of conspiracy, this theme comes up time and again. "I was chosen by an angel to bring these words to you," or "the fate of the world depends on me so I'm not afraid the CIA will harm me for telling you this," or "I am really of alien birth, part human, but also something more than human" and so on.

The megalomania of many conspiracy theorists is second only to the many glaring discrepancies of fact enshrined in their theories. Like the reveries of paranoid psychotics, the tales of overarching evil, no matter how outlandish, do often have a striking cohesiveness to them, at least at first blush, very much like the scary tidings of the Book of Revelation that, even after almost two millennia, have yet to appear as foretold.

But inevitably a second and more critical appraisal begins to expose weak spots, cracks in the woodwork and frays in the weave, and soon the whole flaming four-stroke-cycle mojo begins to come apart. The bottom line on most conspiracy theories I've looked at is they just don't make sense, they don't hold up under scrutiny. The only available "facts" are really factoids, and I've found few works that meet even basic criteria for scholarship. Mostly what's out there is infojunk, infojunk and more infojunk.

In a lot of ways the more far-out and fringe conspiracy spiels remind me of the relentless process of dismantling reality used by cults to brainwash recruits and keep indoctrinated members in line. The whole feel and flavor of many theories, taken as a whole, is distinctly cultish. Once the infodrug gets hold of the mind, and all the victim hears over and over again, is the same line, the mind no longer screens out fact from falsehood and the poison takes effect.

By another way of looking at it, today's conspiracy theories may be tantamount to modern myths. The CIA instead of the Olympian gods controlling man's fate. Aliens instead of Set, Horus and Osiris, Zeus, Athena and Apollo. Myths of mankind's interaction with higher—or at least other—forces have been around since prehistory. I'm not disturbed by this trend to mythologize as much as by the content of today's info-myth cycles.

If the strange worlds of conspiracy land are really Daliesque reflections of our own society and culture, as all myths are cultural reflections, then we may well be on the brink of catastrophe. That's the crux—it's not the aliens, the evil gods, the time warpers, the blood ghouls, the mindmuckers, the slimesuckers who are making us hate each other as much as we seem to do, but it is we, ourselves, who are revealing the spiritual poverty of our lives by the twisted, nightmarish evil we spin into warped tales of conspiracy.

Is society controlled, even manipulated by powerful

forces? *Cela va sans dire* (hell, yeah). There hasn't been a civilization on the face of the earth where the few at the top haven't conspired to control the multitudes at the bottom. It's basic Learyesque mammalian politics. This country is no exception.

It's just that the grade-school conditioning about how godlike we Americans are, how noble and how great our institutions, how mighty our science and industry, and conversely how corrupt and impoverished just about everyone else on earth is, has finally begun to wear off after Vietnam, Watergate, Iran-Contra, insider trading, Abscam, Heaven's Gate, Nazi gold at the Federal Reserve Bank of New York, Monica Lewinsky, the Florida ballot recount and a thousand other unpleasant revelations, large and small, that have shattered post–World War II notions of infallibility that were once held by most Americans as unshakable articles of faith.

The imperfections, the hypocrisy, the corruption, the scams, the bullshit—all of it was always there, but nobody wanted to look at it square-on. Today it's just the opposite. People can't help looking and are scared by what their eyes behold. My position is that conspiratorial cabals are as much a functional part of society as are flags, megacorps, toxic waste, paper money and presidential groupies.

But as is the case with so many things, right and wrong, good and bad, sick and well, it all adds up to a question of degree. When conspiratorial modes of dealing with situations become business-as-usual, when the cult of secrecy and lies becomes the preferred mode of interpersonal and intergroup dealings, when the machinations of the few at the top become the style of doing business for those in the middle and bottom, then a cancer of sorts has spread through the body politic and it must be rooted out before it begins to mutate into the HIV of totalitarianism, as happened in Germany and Italy seventy-odd years ago, and in Russia twenty-odd years before that.

Though not a fin de siècle movement, National Socialism in post–World War I Germany also played on mass distrust in authority and an unstable social order to fan the flames of fascist revolution that swept the Sieg-Heilers to power.

The Nazi party used conspiracy theory to its maximum advantage, as a lash to whip the German masses into a frenzy of fear and hatred and springboard the führer to absolute power in a totalitarian state. Hitler had railed against conspiracies led by communists, Jews, Catholics, capitalists and Gypsies, among others, in his quest for the chancellorship. The Nazis were masters of disinformation and used it as effectively to serve their sinister ends as they used truncheons, rifles and marching hordes of jackbooted storm troopers.

Once Germany's highest office was his, Hitler needed "proof" of the grand conspiracy to help him consolidate power and mobilize the German masses to serve his long-range ambitions. Soon after attaining office, on the cold night of February 27, 1933, Hitler got his proof when the Reichstag, or German Parliament building, burned to the ground.

A young Dutch communist, Marinus van der Lubbe,

confessed to the dastardly deed, and said he'd acted out of political motives. Since van der Lubbe was also a Jew—i.e., a member of a group that Der führer claimed was behind every sinister event in the universe—Hitler's warnings of a conspiracy seemed vindicated, and he used the Reichstag fire as a pretext to suspend all vestiges of German democracy and substitute an ironfisted Nazi totalitarian rule in its stead.

In the fire's wake, ratzi storm troopers staged mass arrests of suspected communists and subjected them to sham trials and summary executions. But another blood purge, this time of supposed "traitors" in Nazi ranks, was soon to follow, during and after the so-called Night of the Long Knives in June 1934.

Whether or not the Nazis had in fact staged the Reichstag blaze using van der Lubbe as what we would call a "patsy" today is still being debated.

What is much more certain is that throughout this period Soviet leader Joseph Stalin and German führer Adolf Hitler acted in accord with a secret pact engineered to actually serve the common interests of both dictatorships, while outwardly Nazis and communists subjected each others' side to bitter attacks. Though each side was dedicated to the other's destruction and well aware that a time would come when they would go to war, neither was strong enough yet to attack the other.

Instead, while a war of words ensued, each side assisted the other in fanning the flames of mutual hatred, fear and anger, while simultaneously keeping the liberal Western democracies on the offensive. All of this took place approximately six years before the official Nazi-Soviet pact of August 1939 that stunned the world in the wake of the Nazi invasion of Poland and paved the way for World War II.

Today, in times far more uncertain and volatile than our leaders are willing to admit, conspiracy theories abound like patches of livid toadstools sprouting in a dung heap after a thunderstorm. Mass media and revolutionary developments in electronic mass communications have meant that the lone Jeremiahs shouting their apocalyptic ravings at the fickle winds are a thing of the past.

On the World Wide Web, where hundreds can surf even low-profile Web pages every day, and high-end sites log thousands of daily hits, conspiracy theories are disseminated at an unbelievable rate. A test search of the phrase "conspiracy theory" on Yahoo! returned 1,052 hits, for example, and another one on Lycos returned a similar number. Moreover, the Web affords the kooks and the crazies equal time to air their messages with more credible spokespersons.

Television coverage in an age where coverage of news events is based more on infotainment value than relevance, and where news reportage seems to become more factoid and tabloid with each passing year, is little better at distinguishing illusion from reality, or inculcating the ability to do this in the minds of the viewing public. The presence on TV of dramatic fiction series that try to simulate a contrived and stilted facade of cinema verité by mimicking the style of documentary coverage also adds to the blurring of distinctions between fiction and reality.

Millions of Americans use television as a window on the world, viewing events through the moronic kaleidoscope tunnel of the TV screen. Once upon a time, most news coverage came from print and required not only literacy, but the ability to think. Postliterate American society, glued to the boob tube like drone bees to a honeycomb, has lost this ability. America has become a sponge, an information sponge if you will, that soaks up electronic infojunk, is squeezed dry, then returns to soak up more again. Sponges can't think, they can only absorb and dribble. Sponges can't distinguish truth from falsehood. Sponges just lay there on the counter, waiting to be soaped up and used.

When things begin to look unreal on TV they also begin to look artificial in the world that surrounds these chronic viewer-sponges. The universe becomes a lie within a lie and the human mind becomes lost in a wilderness of mirrors, to use T. S. Eliot's well-known phrase.

But at the same time it's also clear to any sane mind that many conspiracies and the cover-ups that often follow them as attempts to erase their tracks are all too real.

Watergate was real. Richard Nixon sanctioned a cover-up of the break-in at the Democratic Party headquarters, and some, including former White House Chief of Staff H. R. Haldeman, even suggest Nixon instigated the burglary from the start. The CIA's Cointelpro program, where the agency violated the terms of the 1947 National Security Act prohibiting it from domestic covert activities, was also real.

The John F. Kennedy assassination was real, obviously, but the evidence of a massive cover-up is also too overwhelmingly real to be ignored by this point in history. UFO phenomena and alien-human interaction may also have the weight of anecdotal evidence on their side. And the list goes on. The blurring of reality and the incontrovertible fact of some modern-day conspiracies are mutually supporting and foster a building atmosphere of paranoia. They reinforce one another, and like masses of hot air meeting cold in the upper reaches of the atmosphere, set into motion a churning, spiraling vortex of escalating unreason, rumor and lies. Some even claim that this chain of events is deliberate, indeed manufactured by shadowy puppet masters in and outside government to keep the population in a constant state of panic and to rob us of our ability to think and question, dumbing us down by overloading our minds and substituting regimentation and docility in the place of mental engagement and intellectual independence.

Whether conspiracy theories are wrong or right, their very currency has important consequences for everyone. If there are segments of society with little or no accountability, it robs the rest of us of freedom and introduces a way of life based on deception and fraud. Once telling lies becomes a way of life and doing business, once it's taken for granted that nothing anybody tells you—whether it be the president, your doctor, or the mechanic fixing your car—can be wholly believed, then we live in a Kafkaesque world of increasing insanity, unreality and amorality.

Another consequence of the lie as a way of life is that it pumps up the level of rage in society. A person lied to is a person used, and a person used soon becomes a person angry. Multiply that anger by a factor of around two hundred million and you get a compelling explanation for the level of hostility on the roads and in the marketplace that has never before been greater. It explains a great deal about why a total stranger will whip out a handgun and shoot another total stranger on the highway for cutting in front of him, or why a schoolboy will tote a rifle to school with him one day and gun down other schoolchildren eating lunch in the cafeteria.

It's not so much that we can't live in a world of lies. On the contrary, I think we need to believe in certain lies as much as in certain truths. Myths are forms of lies, and they sometimes enable us to transcend our limitations and live up to ideals that might be more heroic than we might be willing to dare realize had we looked the truth squarely in the face. By the same token, the governors of nations have throughout history concealed unpleasant and unworkable facts from the governed, and often these secrets have worked toward the greater good.

We all recognize this, and there was a time when we unquestionably accepted that if a president or other national authority figure lied to us it was probably in our best interest and we chose to be deceived. Most of us instinctively followed this course during Desert

13

Storm, for example. Whether we believed the flimsy pretext of "liberating Kuwait" from Iraqi despotism or not, we accepted the glitzy logos and slick public relations campaign in place of an unprecedented wartime news blackout.

Most of us—and I include myself in this number—walked around with a knowing smirk and a contact high, willing to wink at what was going on as long as Our Side was finally winning one for a change. Had the war taken a different course or lasted considerably longer than it did, this attitude surely would have changed dramatically. But the war ended quickly and—it seemed at the time—favorably, and for a brief while the nation's faith in the wisdom of its leadership rose to a level rivaling that of a past generation.

So lies and cover-ups in and of themselves are not necessarily bad. It's when the lies are compounded, when they serve the interests of a select few at the expense of the majority and when the process of conspiracy and cover-up begins to assume a life of its own that things begin to fall apart. Just as the human body can sustain small numbers of germs and still remain healthy but becomes sick when the bacteria multiply, so the body politic suffers when conspiracies take the place of open government and the free dissemination of information.

This book is my personal list of what I think are the major-league conspiracies and cover-ups that affect our lives, a hip-pocket Baedeker to the twilight zone, a street map to the unexplained, a guidebook to the lair of the Minotaur. I don't pretend to be a conspiracy freak or cover-up expert, or that I've spent years studying the phenomenon. I haven't, since I have better things to do, like playing my guitar and loading my Uzi.

And even if I were a champion conspiracy head, the scope of the book would be far too narrow to warrant going into extreme detail. Even a single sector of the conspiracy map could easily take up a book in itself. My main purpose is to spin out some of the prevailing conspiracy theories in a way I hope can contribute fresh insight, and also to ask the right questions. I believe some theories have weight, some have more weight then others and some, frankly, are a total joke. You'll see what I mean.

That's all for now. I've got to go quick because I can sense them coming to get me. Meet me later and we'll talk some more. You know the place, and I already gave you the code words. In the meantime don't say anything to anybody. It might blow our covers and compromise the entire operation!

First Arkon and Primal Poobah Dave,
Supreme Meister of the Thirteenth Seal,
Hotel Nirvana, Dream Street, Planet Earth

architects of NWO by conspiraholics). This, and the establishment of FEMA, the Federal Emergency Management Agency, which has been granted sweeping powers during emergencies, is claimed to underpin the conspiracy's success.

The Oklahoma City and World Trade Center bombings and the nefarious Unabomber were all manufactured by the conspiracy to lend public support for draconian measures to erode constitutional guarantees, continues the NWO theme song. More such stage-managed catastrophes (the latest at this writing being the destruction of the World Trade Center) will take place as time goes by, building up the level of paranoia and simultaneously eroding freedoms.

When the final crisis emerges—there are disagreements about precisely what form it will take, but it will be something major—FEMA's sweeping powers will be summarily invoked, the nation's political and financial elite spirited to secret facilities and the machinery of suppression, disruption, death and enslavement will be finally and firmly put in place. The New World Order will then have begun.

After the New World Order is imposed, the United States as we know it will effectively cease to exist. In fact, all countries will effectively cease to exist. Instead, the world will be governed by a supreme cadre of power elites, among whom would be members of the Council on Foreign Relations (CFR) and Trilateral Commission (TLC), the Bilderberger Group (an international society notable to conspiracy buffs for the membership of archfiend Henry Kissinger) and sundry other supercadres of plotters, all of them the contemporary avatars of the ancient Bavarian Illuminati of Adam Weishaupt or the Masonic orders, which established the plan in the first place.

The rest of humanity will serve their new masters in various slave capacities, ranking higher or lower depending on caste. Those who resist will be killed, en masse if necessary, with Waco and Ruby Ridge being cited as dress rehearsals for the coming genocide practiced by them-uns against us-uns. Those at the bottom will be worked to death performing dangerous manual labor, used in genetic experiments and for blood sport, or even as food sources for the NWO's extraterrestrial partners. Most uncool, no?

Obviously, troops, this is about as fringe as you can get, especially when certain of the more esoteric aspects of NWO theory, such as AIDS being a bioweapon concocted of alien glandular secretions, Tesla's earthquake machine being behind the 1994 San Francisco quake and spy satellites taking pictures of us right through the walls of our bathrooms, are taken into consideration.

I also pick up a definite sense of brain dysfunction when I read the bulk of the NWO literature posted on Web sites devoted to conspiracy theory. By comparison with other conspiracy literature, even that concerning alien abductions, for example, NWO posts are mostly rants from rural fascists who carry on about the government's plan to destroy our minds, yet can't even seem to muster the wherewithal to correctly spell "government."

There's also a great deal of religious posturing and declarations that patriotism, love of America and other flag-waving hyperbole lie behind the poster's decision to come forward and face possible death for revealing the terrible secrets to which he or she has fallen privy. This only bolsters my view that to these right-wing fanatics the U.S. Constitution is tantamount to the Koran to fundamentalist Shiite terrorists—in short, a sanctimonious cover for far darker motives.

Some of the stuff is lucid, but only up to a certain point. You begin to say to yourself, "Hmm . . . maybe there's something to this whole ball o'wax after all." But only for a minute or so. Then inevitably the apocalyptic claims veer off into the twilight zone with the citation of a statistic that you recognize as being very obviously fabricated or a line of reasoning that is completely illogical.[1]

There is also something I consider very important missing from every argument for the NWO theory: a credible motive for the plan of world domination.

Why would super-powerful elites, who today and throughout history have wielded incredible power and who enjoy incredible wealth and privilege, want to risk failure just to get more of what they already possess? How could a scheme of such prodigious complexity,

---

1. See Richard Hofstadter's classic work *The Paranoid Style in American Politics* (Knopf, 1965) for more on this phenomenon.

one involving members of secret societies across the globe, coordinate itself? You put two tort attorneys together in one room and you've got yourself a surefire furball, and yet we're told that twenty Stalins and thirty Hitlers will coordinate a worldwide operation to enslave a billion people without a hitch.

How would these doomsmeisters carve up the New World Order in such a way to prevent utter chaos from resulting from such a destabilizing experiment? Why would an NWO conspirator in, say, Russia, consent to share power with his fellow fascist puppet master in America and other parts of the world in a one-world government where all of today's nations were abolished? Has any dictator in the history of the world ever acted that way, that is, counter-nationalistically? Why should this new breed of Genghis Khans prove any different?

It's one thing for a Hitler or a Stalin to march their countrymen to war and even to massacre millions of their nation's citizenry in the name of absolute power, but it's an entirely different thing for a group or organization that does not possess supreme dictatorial authority to do the same.

Furthermore, at no time in human history has a dictator succeeded in committing genocide on more than a single segment of his own nation. Not even Stalin, whose murder of an estimated million Ukrainians was accepted by White Russians as a form of what we would today call "ethnic cleansing." Today, the genocide in Bosnia-Herzegovina has followed this same pattern. Hitler proved that genocide is mainly a commodity for export; it only works back home with a relatively small scapegoat group, and the NWO conspiracy would need to cut across a wide swath of the U.S. population in order to achieve its ends.

The arguments given for the emergence of a New World Order remind me of the justifications Inspector Clouseau gave in one of the Pink Panther movies concerning why he was doggedly chasing after a certain criminal master brain that logic showed could not possibly exist. Each time Chief Inspector Dreyfus shot down Clouseau's dumb reason with a completely logical question, Clouseau came up with a retort that was even dumber.

"Why would he murder a Cossack?" asked the chief inspector in a fit of facial apoplexy.

"Because he's a homicidal maniac," replied a completely deadpan Clouseau.

And so on.

Like Clouseau (and like paranoid schizoids, for that matter), those in favor of NWO conspiracies show a tendency to screen out anything that contradicts their obsessive monomaniacal viewpoint or doesn't feed its unreality. They also remind me a great deal of Nazis, who are, in fact, very strong proponents of New World Order conspiracy theories.

For Hitler and his crew, there was a Bolshevik/capitalist/Jewish conspiracy that was out to destroy Germany and enslave her "helpless" people. That conspiracy was already at work in the part of Czechoslovakia known as the Sudetenland, where "concentration camps" for Germans were supposedly being built, at least according to prewar propaganda. So Hitler and his storm troopers needed to save the day and "liberate" the Sudeten Germans by goose stepping into Czechoslovakia like Saddam Hussein marched into Kuwait.

Today, neo-Nazis and nazoid militia movements have adopted the New World Order conspiracy line with the same gusto that Adolf and his merry band of brownshirts did sixty-odd years ago. It's pretty much the same line—directed toward the same end—only with words like "Jew" and "communist" replaced by more contempo phrasewords.

I believe, however, that NWO conspiracy wackos do have value as a kind of barometer of what is really happening in our society. Just as a dipstick thrust into motor oil comes out either dirty or clean and can be a useful gauge of what's happening inside the engine, NWO theory might be painting a picture of what's happening in places normally obscured from collective view. It's possible that what today's wannabe Himmlers perceive, albeit through a glass darkly, is a dim picture of a thing they called "the ground truth" in the Gulf.

Take underground bases, for example. Although many claims may be exaggerated, there is no doubt that such bases do in fact exist (see chapter on secret bases). There is equally no doubt that these bases are extensive and constructed to function as self-contained hideaways for the political, military and, to a lesser extent, intellectual elite in the event of nuclear catastrophe or other form of major national emergency.

It is also perfectly likely that detention facilities for the containment of millions of prisoners have been

constructed on these bases and that transportation facilities exist to shuttle the prisoners to the bases when
the time comes in support of somebody in government's draconian emergency planning. I would con-
cede that once detained at these facilities in a time of
future crisis, some or many of the prisoners might indeed be killed, also according to the meister plan.

However, I don't believe that the fact that such facilities may exist equals proof that ipso facto a far-
reaching New World Order conspiracy exists, only that
factions of government could be taking measures
against a time when some form of apocalyptic disaster
might strike the nation. This disaster might be as cosmic as an alien invasion or a runaway asteroid, but it
could be something just as destructive, albeit far more
prosaic, that U.S. war planners fear they see just over
the horizon.

This could be the proliferation of nuclear weapons
into the hands of Third World nations, global criminal
organizations, terrorist organizations, and other nonstate actors, such as corporate cartels.

Nuclear weapons development has been almost completely black, that is, almost no public disclosure or
congressional oversight has ever existed to cover it.
Because of this, technological innovations that have
produced smaller and smaller nuclear devices have proceeded unchecked for decades.

Today, nuclear weapons in the multi-kiloton to one-
megaton range—powerful enough to destroy the heart
of a city—have been reduced to the size of a narrow
cylinder that can be carried in an overnight bag and

planted virtually anywhere. A nuclear terrorist could leave one, or several, on a subway train and make the 1993 World Trade Center bombing look like a marshmallow roast.

Tomorrow, say by the year 2015, the Russians or the French or the Chinese will be selling cruise missiles that will outperform the legendary Tomahawk of Desert Storm fame to any country with the money to buy them. Such nuclear cruise missile technology—stealthy, deadly and almost impossible to track and kill—in the hands of tomorrow's Saddam Husseins or Osama bin Ladens means that the technology of nuclear holocaust will have reached about the same accessibility level as the mainframe computer. Just about any nation could afford it, and virtually anything might lead certain despots to use this awesome weaponry.

Pentagon war planners know this fact only too well, and recent white papers, such as *Transformation in Defense,* released in December 1997, make their concerns only too clear. Should a nuclear attack on a major U.S. urban center, such as New York, Boston or San Francisco, materialize, computer war game scenarios have predicted that masses of refugees would then converge on outlying areas. Many would be sick, all would be hungry and desperate, and in many cases also armed.

The National Guard and other military forces ordered to deal with this terrible exodus would then be faced with the task of sorting out the mess, contending with the masses of survivors and restoring civil order at any price. Their prime directive would be to insure the continuity of the U.S. government and national and international communications links from government transmission nodes at any and all costs.

To military planners, accustomed to thinking in terms of casualty rates, rescue and rehabilitation of the affected population would be of secondary concern. Many individuals might conceivably be killed in the name of protecting the majority from illness, whereas others could be quarantined for indefinite periods of time.

It's my opinion that this is closer to the true doomsday scenario that lies behind the existence of many of the sightings of black helicopters, strange war games and even evidence of underground detention facilities in connection with NWO conspiracy theory. It's also entirely possible that elements of a complex, multilevel bureaucracy are following secret agendas and that contingency plans for emergency management exist that could easily enough—perhaps even deliberately—be abused under the proper set of circumstances.

But this isn't a New World Order, it's just plain, old-fashioned, fascist coup d'etat, and to me, that's frightening enough in itself.

IMPACT ANALYSIS

Even if NWO conspiracy theories are wrong, we need to be on guard against the abuse of our civil liberties by an unfeeling bureaucratic elite that would sacrifice the many to safeguard the few. The many did not question the need to shed their lifeblood on the shores of Anzio,

Salerno, Normandy, in the jungles of Vietnam or on the sands of Iraq and Kuwait, and our very existence as a republic is based upon the sacredness and equality of every individual life. Let us be vigilant, but let us soberly weigh the facts before we jump to conclusions concerning New World Order plans.

Dirty Money

If there's any doubt concerning the importance of the almighty buck, consider the almighty fact that the dollar sign is made up of the two letters *U* and *S* superimposed on one another, proof positive that money and the United States are synonymous.

In fact, the dollar bill has itself been the subject of scrutiny by numerous conspiracy theorists, the kind who see Klan symbols on Marlboro hardpacks and road maps to the New World Order on the flip side of Cheerios boxes. These same persons have pointed out the Masonic and Bavarian Illuminati symbology found on the dollar bill, which does in fact seem to have some weird symbols when you get right down to it.

The word "one" in large capital letters dominates the

reverse of the bill and has above it the inscription, "In God We Trust," which was added only as recently as 1963, according to *From Rocks to Riches,* a publication of the Federal Reserve Bank of New York.

To either side of this word are representations of the back and front of the Great Seal of the United States. At the left, the reverse of the Great Seal shows a small pyramid, truncated near the apex that, surrounded by a mysterious halo, seems to float above the lower portion.

This small pyramid contains a human eye and is an ancient symbol of Masons, Copts and Illuminati, to name but a few. Above this are the Latin words *Annuit Coeptis,* which mean "God has favored our undertakings" and is an adaptation from Virgil's martial epic *The Aeneid,* which tells of the mythical founding of ancient Rome by the survivors of the Trojan War.

In a banner that runs below the bottom of the broad base of the pyramid are the words *Novus Ordo Seclorum,* which, also from the writings of Virgil (in this case his *Eclogues*), literally means, "A new order of the ages" but might just as accurately be translated as— you guessed it, partner—"New World Order."

On the right is the front of the Great Seal, on which the American eagle is depicted with an olive branch and a brace of arrows clutched in its talons and another banner clutched in its beak. This banner also bears a Latin inscription, the familiar *E Pluribus Unum,* which in English means, "Out of many, one," and is, of course, the motto of the United States of America.

On the front of the dollar bill is a portrait of George

Washington, considered by many historians to have been a member of a secret Masonic lodge. To Washington's right is the seal of the U.S. Treasury with renditions of a balancing scale, a latchkey and a chevron containing thirteen stars, one for each original American state.

The former two images are also ancient symbols of Masonic and other secret societies. Until 1996 the seal also bore a Latin inscription, which was then replaced with the current "The Department of the Treasury 1789" inscription.

There are other aspects of the symbolism of the dollar, including the color green (said to be a color associated with aliens, for example), that do indeed make it a strange piece of paper money, especially in an age where most of the world's currencies have been completely overhauled with anticounterfeiting measures, including holograms, metallic interweaves and microprinting schemes that are not reproducible on color copiers.

The U.S. greenback has changed very little since the original issue of the first Federal Reserve notes back in 1914, the year the U.S. government went from a gold-backed currency to paper or fiat currency. The bizarre floating pyramid with the phrase "God has favored our undertakings" surmounting the broad base of the pyramid that covers the phrase "New World Order" seems especially weird.

If you have the right turn of mind, it could be read as saying, "The people at the top—the 5 percent of society who control 70 percent of the wealth—have

God on their side, while those making up the broad base of the social pyramid—the other 95 percent of the population—will be subjected to their control in the New World Order. The rulers at the top are ever-vigilant and are cut off from the many at the bottom, who live their lives in comparative darkness." (It could also be saying, "Money talks and bullshit walks," of course.)

But here's what the Federal Reserve Bank has to say about the subject in the same 1992 pamphlet cited earlier: The Fed claims that *Annuit Coeptis* is Latin for "He has favored our undertakings." The phrase has thirteen letters, a reference to the original thirteen states. The pyramid represents "material strength and an enduring foundation for future growth." It is unfinished, indicating perfection as a goal to be achieved.

The thirteen levels of the pyramid represent the thirteen original states, and the individual blocks represent local government. The "Eternal Eye of God" is placed above the pyramid "to symbolize the spiritual over the material." The phrase *Novus Ordo Seclorum* means "A new order of the ages" and has no sinister connotations.

As to the front of the Great Seal, the olive branch and brace of arrows in the bird's talons symbolize a desire for peace but preparedness for war, if necessary, while the eagle's head, representing the executive branch, faces toward the olive branch, indicating a desire for peace (note the double meaning of the word "branch").

The phrase *E Pluribus Unum*, meaning "Out of

many, one," is simply a statement of national unity (the phrase has thirteen letters, corresponding with the thirteen arrows, olive branches and other numerical symbols found on the dollar representing the thirteen original states).

So there you go. Like so many things, conspiracy can often be in the eye of the beholder. Is the glass half full or half empty? Is the dollar an in-your-face boast by the Conspiracy or just a harmless medium of exchange? At this point, the only thing about the dollar I'm absolutely certain of is that I like having as many as possible on me at all times, in fifties and hundreds, if you please. Cash may be strange, but not having cash makes life a lot stranger, and that's no spit.

Conspiracy theorist Robert Anton Wilson has stated that money functions as a surrogate for the neurological pack bond or tribal imprinting of a precapitalist society. William S. Burroughs likened money to heroin, an addictive substance whose absence creates withdrawal-like symptoms in citizens of capitalist societies who must have a regular "money fix" in order to survive.

Society conditions its citizens by controlling the accessibility of money on the basis of how well an individual conforms to society's dictates, continues this argument. Those who are most obedient get the most money; those who fit in least suffer money-deprivation anxiety, and, like heroin addicts, sometimes even death as a result of a total cutoff of their money supply. As Jack London once wrote, "Capitalism has its own heaven and its own hell, and these are wealth and poverty."

New World Order conspiracy buffs believe that both paper money and metal coinage will be declared illegal for all but the elite and that microchip implants or microchip-enhanced ID cards will very soon be issued to the citizenry in their place toward a totally cashless society.

The chips would contain not only information about how much credit the individual had available—in short, comprising his/her electronic "bank account"—but also enable all vital information about the individual to be instantly scanned by the controlling elite. If a person failed to toe the line, his chip would be deprogrammed of money and there would be no way to pay his bills or even buy groceries. This would be the twenty-first century analog of the public pillory, stocks or other barbarous punishments for "troublemakers" of past ages. (I say, as long as there are still old ladies I can mug in the park, no problem.)

So much for the mythology, symbolism and even inherent conspiracy of the money system. There may be some reason to doubt that money is the source of evil that many believe it to be. Yet there is not a shred of doubt that money and finance have been the basis for some of the most nefarious and well-documented conspiracies since time immemorial.

A number of these have taken place in our century with the full involvement of the U.S. government and the governments of its closest allies. These conspiracies have had worldwide economic consequences that continue to the present day and will have impact long into this century.

Among them is the Nazi-American money conspiracy of World War II, which, among other things, has led to the coverup of millions of dollars in gold looted from victims of Nazi oppression and hidden in Swiss banks until 1997.

"It is estimated that the gold in the vault represents a significant portion of the gold that has been mined throughout history," states another Federal Reserve Bank of New York publication, *The Key to the Gold Vault.*

The pamphlet goes on to talk about how some of the gold may have come from ancient coins, or the tombs of the pharaohs or from hoards of New World treasure brought to Queen Isabella by Columbus, or may even have been spirited out of Europe during World War II to keep it away from Hitler.

One important source for the gold that the pamphlet fails to mention, however, is the dental work, eyeglass frames, jewelry and other personal effects of the six to twelve million people liquidated by the Nazis during the Second World War. Now how could they have forgotten that, eh, troops?

Even when I took a tour of the Federal Reserve Bank of New York in 1993 and stood in front of this huge wire mesh cage stacked from floor to ceiling with golden "Hershey bars" bearing the heraldic eagle of the Third Reich, nobody was willing to acknowledge that the Fed was holding millions in Nazi gold!

Since the vault's storage areas bear no names, only numbers, of the client states that actually own the gold, Fed personnel would only tell me that it belonged to "an unspecified European nation." (Sure.) When I pressed them further, it was suddenly "closing time" and I was ushered out onto the grim streets of lower Broadway, soon to drown my sorrows in a disgusting orgy of Chinese food consumption.

When I approached publishers with proposals for fiction and nonfiction books based on what I'd just seen, nobody was interested. Here was millions of dollars in Nazi gold sitting plunk in the middle of Manhattan and nobody much cared. Like this very book on conspiracies—which I proposed around 1993 and was contracted for only in 1998—the paperwork went back into my files (you've no doubt heard of the place where the sun never shines—well, that's my filing cabinet).

Then—surprise, surprise—in 1997 the story concerning the Nazi gold finally "surfaced." The Swiss, it seems, had not been all bread, chocolate and Alpine Lace cheese during the war. Their vaunted neutrality was a sometime thing, especially when it came to their national pastime—hoarding other peoples' money.

During the war, over $300 million in plundered gold flowed into banking houses in the Swiss financial center of Zurich. The looted gold came in by truck and rail in the form of bars formed from the melted-down gold of death camp victims. It arrived by secret courier and by diplomatic pouch. It even arrived by a fleet of phony Red Cross ambulances, according to some accounts, set up in a scheme by remnants of the Nazi SS. It arrived by many means and was placed in numbered accounts by the "Gnomes of Zurich" who did business with anybody and asked few questions.

But Nazi gold did not just flow into Switzerland's major banking centers. It also flowed into the United States by way of the Federal Reserve Bank of New York, which under its charter with the U.S. government, then as well as now, is responsible for international monetary transactions.

According to reports in the Bonn, Germany–based newspaper *Die Woche* in 1997, documents found in the U.S. National Archives revealed transfers of $128 million in gold from Swiss banks to banks in the U.S. early in the war. The Fed of New York also authorized transfers of millions in gold from German-occupied France to Eva Peron's Argentina (don't cry for Juan, he didn't count for spit) and various other countries.

The U.S. Treasury Department, as other branches of government including the White House and State Department, was aware of the transactions at all times. It had to be, since the Nazi gold was literally staring everybody in the face since day one.

You see, transfers of gold are not always made physically, especially in time of war. More frequently these transfers exist only on balance sheets with so-many dollars, francs, deutsche marks, rubles or yen moved from one account to the other.

The gleaming, yellow Hershey bars need never leave

their wire mesh cages deep within the basement level of the Fed in order for millions to flow from one country to the next. All it takes is a flick of the pen. Thus, the millions of dollars in gold bars stamped with the heraldic eagle of the Third Reich are still sitting somewhere in the basement of the Federal Reserve Bank of New York to this very day, awaiting the disposition of claims by nazidom's victims and their descendents.[1]

Why did the United States government sanction the traffic in bloodstained gold? Some of the justifications given for the transfers have been concern for Nazi retaliation against captured British and American soldiers during the war and the stabilization of the postwar world after the fighting ceased.

Well, maybe. At least the explanations *sound* reasonable. On the other hand, there's another source from which Uncle Sam got untold millions in gold, gems, currency and other valuables that originally came from the dental work, fingers and fleeced pockets of the millions of "subhumans" that Adolf's ratzis shoved pellmell into the gas chambers.

This source was the hoard of hidden SS treasure that was the subject of a feverish hunt by U.S. Seventh Army military intelligence (G-5) after the German surrender.

G-5 had learned that *Reichsführer* Heinrich Himmler, leader of the SS, had ordered the burial of a vast treasure trove as the Reich went under, but Himmler

---

1. This gold is separate from millions in Swiss bank accounts that are also being sought by claimants to World War II funds.

ate a cyanide breath mint before he could be interrogated, and the secret of the treasure died with him. Nevertheless, it was suspected that the cache was to be found somewhere in the rugged mountain country of Taxenbach, Austria, where other Nazi stashes had already been discovered.

Ultimately, a series of leads brought investigators to one Walter Reisinger, an ex–SS *Ortsgruppenleiter,* who was a native of the region and a mountaineer as well. Reisinger's testimony marked the end of the money trail, and an estimated $25 million (in 1945 dollars) fell into the hands of the U.S. military government in Germany as a result.

After that, the Nazi spoils simply disappeared, and though it's suspected that the proceeds ended up in the U.S. Treasury, the Treasury Department has never acknowledged having received any of the money.

Yet Seventh Army records do show that the loot was in fact recovered. So what happened to it?

The consensus is that the SS treasure went into covert funds for use by U.S. intelligence operations directed against the Soviets in Europe during the cold war, and also to finance the Gehlen Organization—the rent-a-Gestapo network staffed by ex–SS officers and funded by the CIA to perform intelligence work in postwar Europe—a large part of that anti-Soviet effort in the opening years of superpower confrontation.

Keeping the existence of the captured spoils secret from Holocaust survivors who might have legitimate claims on the treasure was yet another reason for the coverup. As the saying goes, out of sight, out of mind.

Finally, it's also suspected that a substantial portion of the booty was simply stolen by Allied personnel who took the adage "to the victor belong the spoils" to heart, even if those spoils came from somebody's grandmother's eyeteeth.

But there were other issues related to money transactions between the United States and her putative enemies during the Second World War, including a policy of "business as usual" by a corporate, political and financial elite among American, British and German players that transcended national hostilities. As startling as they undoubtedly are, revelations concerning Nazi gold are just the tip of the iceberg, the visible portion of an even greater conspiracy involving international wealth and power.

In his book *Trading with the Enemy,* Charles Higham has used the term "the Fraternity" to connote the brotherhood of highly placed conspirators in business and government who collaborated in making certain that their economic interests continued unaffected despite differing political ideologies and the fact that their countries happened to be at war at the time. Membership in the Fraternity included powerful players in the United States, Great Britain and Germany, as well as in France, Spain, Argentina and other nations fighting in World War II on opposite sides.

As might be supposed, the machinations of this brotherhood of greed often resulted in developments that served the wartime good of the enemy while placing their host nation's armed forces in severe danger. The case of tetraethyl lead is one example. Tetraethyl lead was a vital additive to aviation fuel used by the Nazi Luftwaffe. Without it, the planes of the German air force would have been grounded.

According to Higham, three U.S. companies, Standard Oil, Du Pont and General Motors, had the rights to manufacture tetraethyl lead. Despite the fact that withholding supplies of the additive to Hitler would have helped Britain, the Fraternity arranged for five hundred tons to be sold to Germany through Ethyl, the British branch of Standard Oil of New Jersey in 1938, Standard then being a partially owned subsidiary of the giant German chemical and manufacturing firm, I. G. Farben. Another $15 million worth of the additive was sold to the Nazis the following year.

By 1940, thanks to the plentiful stockpiles of tetraethyl lead in the hands of the Third Reich, the German Luftwaffe was able to send its warplanes across the English Channel from bases in occupied France and subject London to the first of what were to be many bombing blitzes. If this weren't bad enough, the Fraternity also secured the sale to another Axis power, Japan, of tetraethyl lead, enabling that country to launch a squadron of warplanes to the U.S. naval base at Pearl Harbor in the most infamous sneak attack in history.

Finally, to add insult to the sins of treachery and venality, the British Royal Air Force, which also looked to Ethyl-Standard for the same additive necessary to produce its own aviation fuel, was in the position of actually paying royalties for use of the fuel additive to Ethyl-Standard. In effect the British were paying royalties on the gas used to put German planes into the air to bomb British cities to rubble! These royalties were kept in trust in Germany by Farben's banks for Standard until the war's end.

Among other Farben connections was the notorious death camp, Auschwitz, where among the tasks of prisoners awaiting inevitable extermination was to toil in manufacturing projects for Farben, such as the work carried out at Farben's synthetic Buna rubber factory at the camp. When the time came for the prisoners to die in the gas chambers, the blue crystals of the insecticide Zyklon-B, a form of prussic acid made by the German Corporation for Pest Control, a Farben subsidiary, were there to help them into the hereafter.

The firm even complied with instructions to remove Zyklon-B's special warning odor so it would be undetectable to doomed arrivals believing they were headed for "the showers." Here, Farben officials briefly hesitated, knowing that there was only one reason for this request, and that was to exterminate human beings. In the end the firm went ahead anyway, and reaped sizable profits from its traffic in death.

While all this was taking place, other Farben subsidiaries were conducting business as usual back in the United States.

Not only did the Fraternity line its pockets while Londoners huddled like rats in the underground tubes as their homes were pounded by German high explosives, and while human zombies took one-way trips up the smokestacks of Auschwitz courtesy of the SS, but its schemes also resulted in repercussions to Americans. Standard oil's tanker fleet was in the business of refueling Nazi U-boats at sea even after America was fighting an undeclared war in the Atlantic to supply the British with arms and other war material. Ironically, the same Nazi submarines that later torpedoed U.S. convoys and sent ships and sailors to the bottom of the sea were kept running smoothly by U.S.-supplied oil.

As the war continued, vital supplies of gasoline and motor oil were withheld from the Allies and provided to Germany instead by the Fraternity. Heavy trucks and other vehicles were also kept as much as possible out of the hands of American and British forces by Fraternity members Henry and Edsel Ford. Ball bearings, critical to the manufacture of a wide range of military components from tank treads to aviation parts, were another vital war commodity that was the subject of numerous efforts to keep Nazi Germany supplied while the Allies faced critical shortages.

The net effect of these machinations could be measured in American blood spilled on beachheads from Salerno to Normandy, in mangled limbs blown off by enemy fire, in young men maimed and crippled for life who believed they were fighting for the highest ideals while members of their own government and industry were selling them out and profiteering on the lifeblood in their veins.

On both sides of the Atlantic, the Fraternity power brokers clearly believed that the führer's vision of a New World Order ruled by a corporate elite was the more viable one, or at least the more profitable one, and to such as they, profits were the bottom line, the only thing that counted. But fascist sympathizers and Nazi lovers did not come only from the ranks of industry, they infested government and intelligence circles as well.

The Dulles brothers, John Foster and Allen, are names synonymous with the Office of Strategic Services (OSS), and later, the CIA and State Department. However, the Dulleses first appear as lawyers representing Fraternity business interests. After the war, they would be instrumental in cutting deals with Nazis escaping down the various "ratlines" set up through the Vatican and intelligence agencies, deals which have repercussions to this very day. One of these deals, with the corrupt (and largely inept) private espionage bureau financed by the CIA called the Gehlen Organization, already mentioned, will be dealt with elsewhere in this book.

Among the most ambitious schemes of the Fraternity during World War II was nothing less than a plan to do away with a man they despised in a way that his closest historical counterpart, Bill Clinton, is despised today by similarly motivated factions.

Though a patrician himself, President Franklin Delano Roosevelt was a staunch opponent of fascism and predatory capitalism whose New Deal stuck like a bone in the throats of the brotherhood of dirty money. By 1934, only a year after Hitler had become the German chancellor, highly placed American economic and political fascists had been engaged in closer and closer dealings with affiliates in Nazi Germany and Fascist Italy. They approved of these fledgling corporate totalitarian states and wanted to see America reorganized along similar lines, with a führer or duce figure at the helm.

The solution was a plan to stage a coup d'etat that would either kill Roosevelt or turn him into a figurehead president who took orders direct from the Fraternity. The coup was to be funded by $3 million raised from the treasuries of backers in U.S. banking and industry and supported by Nazis close to Adolf Hitler.

The plan called for a terrorist strike force trained to overthrow the president and replace Roosevelt with World War I hero General Smedley Butler, a marine commander who had been decorated with two Congressional Medals of Honor.

The conspiracy considered Butler the perfect choice for the new American führer who would succeed FDR. He was a nationally known and admired figure at the time. What's more, he had spoken out publicly against Roosevelt's New Deal. Butler, it seemed, would make the perfect Hitler to enslave the United States.

The only problem with the plan was that Butler himself, a loyal American, wanted nothing to do with the fascist plan. When an emissary sent by the conspirators approached him, he feigned interest and strung them along. On subsequent visits their representative embellished the plan, promising Butler unlimited power and millions that could be his if he only played along.

Once he'd learned the full extent of the coup scheme, however, Butler went to the White House and revealed the entire plot to FDR. But FDR could no sooner dismiss the plotters as lunatics than he could have them arrested and tried for sedition. America was still in the grip of the Great Depression; beset by war clouds gathering over Europe for the second time in a generation, and the native fascists represented some of the most prominent leaders in industry and finance in the country.

Bringing them down could well have caused another Wall Street crash like that of 1929 that helped bring on the Great Depression of the 1930s. In the end, Roosevelt exposed the plot by leaking the story to the media. This led to the establishment of a congressional committee to investigate the charges at which Butler appeared to accuse General Douglas MacArthur of being involved in the plot (not, incidentally, the first time MacArthur's name was used in similar connections).

Although the committee found that "certain persons made an attempt to establish a fascist organization in this country" and was "able to verify all the pertinent statements made by General Butler," none of the accused did any time, even when new data revealed that more than a million supporters of the plot had been ready to stage the coup, and that arms, explosives and ammunition were ready to be made available to them. To this day, the planned coup d'etat is a little known fact of American history.

The secret government of wealth remained active beneath the surface through the war that followed and the postwar years. It was to reemerge from time to time in coverups and scandals that made headlines. But by far the most far-reaching efforts of the Fraternity were revealed in the 1980s when another eruption of economic conspiracy emerged in the form of the institution known as BCCI, the Bank of Credit and Commerce International (which some have alternatively dubbed "the Bank of Crooks and Criminals International").

Before investigators closed BCCI's doors in 1991, the bank had risen from its obscure beginnings in Karachi, Pakistan, to become the world's largest banking institution, with resources totaling into the billions of dollars. In the span of just a few short years BCCI had grown to become a formidable force on the international financial marketplace, principally as a middleman and broker between the petrodollar-rich sheikdoms of the Gulf states and the Western interests they were feverishly buying into.

Investigators in the United States and Europe, which included Interpol and the U.S. Treasury Department, originally began delving into BCCI's banking practices because of the bank's shady technique in acquiring U.S. business interests, including but not limited to banks. In time these multiple investigations produced a growing body of evidence that made clear that BCCI was much more than merely a bank: it was a worldwide supercriminal organization that rivaled, and in many cases exceeded, anything about the fictional Spectre of the James Bond films and novels.

The bank had become a third force, a nonstate political entity with immense global power, almost a secret government whose tentacles reached into the highest centers of the world's leadership. For this reason BCCI was dubbed "the Octopus" by a reporter named Danny Casolaro who was found dead under mysterious circumstances while conducting investigative research for a book on the bank. By whatever name, BCCI became a tool to be used by clandestine factions across the globe in conducting secret operations of various kinds—BCCI specialized in making everything possible, for the right people and at the right price.

One area in which BCCI excelled was in the realm of high-level arms sales, especially sales that involved skirting or circumventing the export restrictions of arms from one country to another. The major arms deals said to have been brokered by BCCI are numerous and involve both Third World nations and large Western countries, including the United States, England, France and the Soviet Union.

Among weapons transactions with which BCCI was deeply involved was the Iran-Contra arms transfers of embargoed U.S. armaments to the Iranians under the Ayatollah Khomeini in exchange for a more lenient policy in the return of hostages held by Shiite Muslim terrorists. It's alleged that BCCI was a major player in the coverup, and that the Iranians got much more than the few superannuated Hawk missiles reported in the press via the transfer. Iran may have received far greater quantities of far superior armaments, including first-line jet fighter aircraft as well as stockpiles of spare parts.

In another bizarre scenario, BCCI came to the aid of Kuwait in the closing days of Desert Storm. As CNN showed the world, a line of Kuwaiti tanks rolled into liberated Kuwait City at the head of the victorious allied column. Yet prior to the Iraqi invasion of Kuwait, the Kuwaitis had no tank force.

So how did they acquire one? Through BCCI, which via its wholly owned tank factory in Yugoslavia, diverted an order of sixty-four M-84 tanks from an unnamed Third World customer to the Gulf. This public service to the emir of Kuwait was performed at nominal cost, which not only included direct shipment to the Gulf, but—since the Kuwaiti army didn't have a single tank driver among its ranks—also supplied Czech tankers who rolled the war wagons into Kuwait city with the waving, smiling Kuwaitis riding on top.

But the weapons program that BCCI was most obsessively devoted to and spared no lengths to pursue was the development of the nuclear bomb for Pakistan. One reason for this is the fact that to all intents and purposes, BCCI and the Pakistani military, intelligence and political infrastructure were so closely linked as to be indistinguishable from one another. BCCI not only funded the Pakistani atomic energy and nuclear weapons manufacturing programs, but its so-called "Black Network"—the dark side of the bank functioning as a paramilitary, intelligence and enforcement arm—staged covert operations designed to channel advanced bomb-making technology into Islamabad.

The Black Network of BCCI had ties to Western clandestine networks, including the CIA, supposedly by a direct link to then-Director William Casey, known for his predilection for back-channel operations. Casey's CIA allegedly did favors for BCCI and the Black Network returned the quid pro quo with assistance in covert operations deemed in CIA interests, such as the already cited Iran-Contra arms diversion gambit. The dark underbelly of the bank was said to let nothing stand in its way, including human life, and there are an estimated sixteen deaths worldwide that are believed to have been directly connected to BCCI's covert operations during the bank's tenure.

IMPACT ANALYSIS

Wealth is the driving force behind nations and power, but it is also a fertilizer for corruption. During and even before World War II, a Fraternity of power brokers sought to enrich itself at America's expense. More recently, BCCI showed that wealth, combined with power, can corrupt virtually anything. While BCCI's doors are now closed, and the last convictions against indicted players in the United States have been turned in, the legacy of corruption that its presence has left behind at the pinnacles of world power will not soon fade away. On the contrary, the success of the BCCI operation in creating a supercriminal organization that reaped billions from arms, drugs, restricted techno-transfers, purloined military secrets and dirty money has probably encouraged other would-be founders of a future supercriminal empire in the twenty-first century.

IV

Gulf War Cover-ups

The war in the Gulf was retrograde in many ways. It marked the largest single deployment of U.S. troops since World War II, as well as a return to a form of coalition-style warfare not witnessed since the great Napoleonic Wars of the late eighteenth and early nineteenth centuries.

It also marked a return to a war culture akin to that of pre-Vietnam days when the American media and public colluded in a see-no-evil, hear-no-evil, speak-no-evil policy of reality management. What the Gulf newsmedia showed us was only what contributed to the perception of a war waged with bloodless, high-tech precision. Presto-chango—the gritty actualities of past wars had almost miraculously become relics of the past.

But the sleight of hand wouldn't have worked without Coleridge's "willing suspension of disbelief" on the public's part, who, like a player in a game of blind man's bluff, eagerly donned the blindfold, was spun around and staggered off in search of truth holding a paper donkey's tail.

Beneath the propaganda and the hype, what was not revealed was another face of war in its oldest and grimmest form. This included some new wrinkles, such as a high casualty rate due to so-called "friendly fire" in several major battlefield encounters. Nor were we told about the continuous snafus in command, the towering rages of commanding general H. Norman Schwarz-kopf, the behind-the-scenes doubts and maneuverings and the less-than-perfect performance record of the incredibly costly high-tech weapon systems, such as Stealth and Patriot, that were portrayed as flawless instruments of surgical destruction, but in fact fell far short of this exalted standard.

At the time the fact that we were actually winning one for a change was so intoxicating that few of us dared to do anything but root for the home team and raise a toast to our fearless leader in the White House. The cool, computer-generated logos on the nightly news helped too—somehow, they made you want to drink a lot of beer.

Of course, the euphoria could have only lasted as long as the war remained sitcom length and we kept on scoring shutouts against Saddam's motley desert-rat army. The minute things would have changed into a two-hour docudrama where the good guys took some hits, the bovine excrement would have begun hitting the whirling blades as it ultimately did during Vietnam.

But even so, the American public paid a price for entering into this unprecedented conspiracy of silence. One immediate aftereffect quickly had an impact on returning Gulf War veterans who began getting sick with a malady that came to be known as Gulf War Syndrome.

It's been believed for some time that more than fifteen thousand U.S. troops in the Gulf were exposed to trace amounts of the nerve agent tabun and the blister agent mustard gas after Iraqi weapons dumps were hit by air strikes during the conflict.

But only in 1996, after years of stonewalling in the face of mounting evidence, did the Pentagon finally acknowledge that Gulf War Syndrome was real and had probably been a result of exposure to toxic chemical warfare agents on the battlefield and that, worse yet, Central Command had known all about it from the word go.

Czech chemical warfare detection teams had been patrolling the northern Saudi desert throughout the war. Their mission was to act as forward observation units to provide advance warning of imminent chemical attack. The Czechs were then, and are now, rated as among the most expert in chemical warfare capabilities in the world, and their detection equipment is considered highly reliable.

In the early days of the war, during the Desert Wind

air strikes on Iraqi military targets, the Czech NBC—nuclear biological and chemical—weapons teams flashed warnings to coalition forces under the unified command of General Schwarzkopf. On those occasions their instruments had detected small quantities of nerve and mustard gas wafting across the border from Iraq into the vicinity of American troops.

Nevertheless, their warnings were ignored by Central Command, the coalition military oversight body. Even as the Czechs rushed to put on their MOPP (mission oriented protective posture) gear—gas masks and chemical warfare suits—after detecting the toxic gas seepage, U.S. troops stationed nearby remained unprotected and unconcerned. They had not been ordered to suit up.

In the years following the war, hundreds of veterans began to complain of medical symptoms of various kinds. At first such claims were dismissed as unrelated to anything that happened in the Gulf. The dismissal was made easier by the mysterious disappearance of a sizable portion of record logs documenting chemical and biological weapons exposure incidents and alerts in the war theater (supporters of the Pentagon view attributed the disappearances to "negligence rather than conspiracy").

In the wake of class action lawsuits and extensive press coverage, the Pentagon later acknowledged that U.S. servicemen may have sustained exposure to low doses of nerve agents during demolition of the arms depot at Kamisiyah, Iraq, in March 1991. But, it added, with a single exception, dosages were too small to have led to sustained health problems. The sole exception was in the case of Army Pfc. David Fisher, who suffered exposure to mustard toxin in liquid form, the Pentagon claimed.

It also seems likely that the effects of the otherwise trace amounts of nerve agent exposure may have been heightened by reactions to pyridostigimine bromide, a partially tested nerve agent vaccine with which some four hundred thousand Gulf War servicemen were injected by U.S. medical teams in a hasty effort to immunize them against the possibility of chemical attack, since Saddam was known to hold massive chemical weapons stocks and had demonstrated his willingness to use them on several previous occasions.

Another aspect of Gulf War Syndrome is the effect of exposure to U.S. ammunition itself, especially a form of tank round made from depleted uranium. Since nuclear reactors generate tons of toxic nuclear waste each year and since disposal of this waste is a growing ecological problem, one use for the waste is in the manufacture of ammunition, especially the form of tank ammunition called kinetic energy (KE) rounds.

These rounds are so named because, while not containing an explosive charge like conventional rounds, they undergo an explosive change of state on striking their target. At the ultrahigh "terminal" velocities of impact, the rounds penetrate tank armor and liquify inside, spraying the interior of tanks with jets of molten metal and fragments of armor plate. Being a superdense material, uranium would make the perfect substance to forge into tank ammunition once its radioactivity had been reduced to non-toxic levels by a chemical process called depletion.

Unfortunately for thousands of Gulf War veterans of several countries, while the depletion process had in theory rendered the ammunition safe to handle, it was still too hot to be handled safely without special protective gear that was not issued to tank crews in the Gulf.

The main reason for the toxicity of the rounds is that while the small amounts of radiation released by the rounds did not pose a significant health risk from contact exposure, particles of radioactive metal dust released in the process of handling did pose a genuine risk when inhaled by unprotected troops.

Here, even a small amount of airborne contaminant in low rad dosages can and did have long-term health consequences. Nor were Gulf War soldiers properly protected or informed about the risks of loading and transporting depleted uranium rounds. The Pentagon's stonewalling on this and other aspects of Gulf War Syndrome is another legacy of the culture of silence that surrounded the prosecution of the war.

As I write this, yet another report on Gulf War Syndrome, this one issued by the Senate, claims there is insufficient evidence to link exposure to nerve agents with the illness, supporting the Pentagon's original claim that no single cause underlies Gulf War Syndrome. The report characterized as "overstated" an estimate that some ten thousand troops were exposed,[1]

---

1. The report's figure.

blaming flawed computer modeling of toxic plumes by CIA analysts and a predisposition to assume a worst-case scenario by investigators reviewing the data.

The report is already being challenged by many, including Senator Arlen Specter, who stated, "My judgment is that nerve gas is a contributing factor to Gulf War illness," adding, "[the Pentagon remains] unprepared for the problems of chemical and biological warfare and what may occur as a result of terrorism."

Gulf War weaponry also figured in another aspect of what we weren't told about Desert Storm—the true performance of the multi-billion-dollar combat systems financed by our taxes on the one hand, and the actual military readiness of the enemy that coalition forces were supposedly facing, on the other.

The much-ballyhooed brilliant weapons systems were the media stars of Desert Storm. Their performance garnered endless superlatives from media spin doctors and self-congratulatory military spokesmen. But the truth about many weapons' performance is very different. The fact is often the direct opposite of the hype.

According to a study by the General Accounting Office (GAO), a congressionally appointed investigatory body with fiscal oversight, which the Pentagon suppressed for years following the war's end, "there was no apparent link between the cost of aircraft and munitions" and "their performance in Desert Storm."

The study, released in 1997, also concluded that performance claims for advanced weapons systems ranging from the F-117 Stealth fighter to the Patriot missile defense system revealed a consistent "pattern of over-statement," as did claims of the accuracy and number of hits scored by laser-guided munitions and other "brilliant" weaponry.

The GAO's findings were echoed by the USAF's own postwar analysis. The air force figures showed that laser- and radar-guided bombs and missiles accounted for only 7 percent of all U.S. explosives dropped in Iraq and Kuwait.

The other 93 percent of munitions strikes were scored by conventional "dumb" iron bombs delivered mainly by cold war–vintage B-52 jet bombers. Ten percent of laser-guided munitions missed their targets, according to the USAF, while 75 percent of dumb munitions did not hit their marks.

In other terms, approximately sixty thousand tons of explosives—about 70 percent of all Desert Storm ordnance—missed their targets completely. And these are data from only two sets of figures. Separate studies were conducted by other U.S. government organizations, including the army and navy, and these confirm and in some cases exceed the USAF and GAO figures.

One weapon system that became a megastar during Desert Storm was the Patriot antimissile system. But in a Massachusetts Institute of Technology analysis of Patriot performance another reality emerged. The MIT analysis showed that the damage per Scud attack was actually higher with Patriot than where there had been no defense at all.

One reason for this debacle is that most Patriot interceptions of incoming Scuds resulted in the breakup, rather than the complete destruction, of the Iraqi missiles. This not only resulted in the creation of chunks of flaming metal debris that rained down on targets like Riyadh and Tel Aviv, but also confounded the Patriot's sophisticated but bug-ridden tracking software. Patriot batteries were only supposed to fire two salvos at any single incoming missile, but the twenty-seven Patriot batteries in Israel and Saudi Arabia often fired as many as ten missiles per incoming Scud.

Consequently, the number of Israeli apartments damaged by Scuds tripled and the number of injuries increased by 50 percent after Patriots were brought into the theater, because falling debris from disintegrating Scuds dispersed damage over a wider area. The damage per site was lighter than a direct hit by a Scud warhead would, of course, have been, but the devastation was more widespread.

Another software bug in the Patriot system was responsible for perhaps the most damaging Scud attack of the entire conflict, the destruction of a U.S. Army barracks housed in a converted warehouse in the Al Khobar suburb of Dhahran. Ironically, the Al Khobar Scud was the last Iraqi missile launched during the war. The failure to intercept the incoming warhead has been attributed to a flaw in the Patriot software that resulted in a timing error that became more pronounced the longer the system was active.

Patriot crews got around the glitch by simply turning their systems off periodically. But the crew manning the Patriot battery in Dhahran on the fateful night of the attack had permitted their system to remain active too long without corrective downtime. The result was that the incoming Scud was invisible to the installation's tracking software. It sailed right in, and hit the barracks, leaving a toll of twenty-eight killed and ninety-eight wounded, all of whom were noncombatant rear-echelon staff. For want of a screen saver, a kingdom fell.

As for the supposed Iraqi threat faced by coalition forces that necessitated the massive buildup of Desert Shield, this too may have been grossly overinflated, although whether deliberately or due to poor intelligence remains a matter still open to question.

Immediately following the Iraqi invasion of Kuwait, the Pentagon claimed Iraqi troop strength estimates in the vicinity of two hundred fifty thousand men and fifteen hundred tanks. But a series of controversial satellite photos purchased from the Russians by one news agency and supposedly of good resolution showed nothing like this in the theater. Revised estimates by Central Command later in the war, and by postwar studies of independent sources, indicated that actual Iraqi troop strength was less than 20 percent of what the brass hats originally claimed was out there.

The Pentagon and the media also built up the fight much like good boxing promoters before a world-class championship bout. Iraq was said to have a heavily fortified system of trenches and bunkers in place, belts of sand berms twelve feet or more in height encircling lethal minefields and oil-filled trenches that would bog

U.S. troops in a quagmire that foretold heavy losses.

There were indeed obstacles and defenses built by the Iraqis, including minefields on the Kuwaiti and Iraqi borders that often posed grave problems when breached by coalition forces, and frequently encountered berms across the desert. There was also an extensive naval minefield surrounding the Kuwaiti shoreline that severely damaged at least two allied naval vessels. But by the time the Desert Wind air strike phase was underway, surveillance data showed allied commanders that the much-feared Iraqi gauntlet of death was nowhere in evidence.

Furthermore, U.S. AirLand battle tactics were designed to bring troops deep behind enemy lines without going directly through such defenses but by going over and around them instead. A head-on assault that would have shoved invasion forces straight through Saddam's meat grinder like the proverbial camel through the eye of a needle was never in the cards at any point.

Just the same, there were several distinctly bloody encounters where U.S. servicemen got themselves badly mauled. Indeed, it was the nature of the fatalities that helped provoke the cover-up to keep the news from the public. On the one hand, the Iraqis sometimes turned out to fight better than we gave them credit for; on the other hand, our own troops were slaughtering each other in friendly fire incidents unprecedented in the history of modern warfare.

Many of the combat deaths in Desert Storm were encountered by General Walter Boomer's marine divisions who were tasked with drawing Iraqi fire by staging a decoy invasion into enemy territory via southern Kuwait—the feint in the renowned "Hail Mary" play. The marines were not only out to lure Saddam's forces into massing in the south while the ground invasion's main thrust came via the north, but also to go after the Iraqi Republican Guard.

In many cases Boomer's hard-chargers met Iraqi counterattacks that, while doomed to failure because of coalition ownership of the air, were nonetheless well-coordinated strikes that wreaked havoc on friendly troops. Such battles did not fit the stereotype of half-naked, Koran-clutching rabble crawling out of crude desert bunkers and doing the "dying cockroach" in surrender to allied troops. On the contrary, the battles demonstrated that we were in a real war in which victory, though perhaps imminent, was by no means guaranteed, and accurate news coverage of these facts might have fed dissent on the home front.

Another major factor in coalition battlefield deaths was fratricide, alternatively known as "blue-on-blue" or friendly fire casualties. These casualties were suffered by a remarkably high percentage of troops in the Gulf theater.

Of the 148 U.S. troops who were killed in action during Desert Storm, 35 were hit by friendly fire. Out of the 467 wounded in action, 72 were wounded by their own side. In other terms this means that 23 percent of U.S. dead and 15 percent of wounded were victims of friendly fire, an extraordinary casualty rate for its type.

Apart from disproving the bloodless war theory pandered by the media, acknowledgment of friendly fire casualties would also have cast doubt on the performance of high-technology weapons systems, because most, if not all these above-mentioned deaths were a result of targeting errors based on costly systems that did not perform as advertised. Where the media only showed high-definition video images of perfect strikes and "good kills," as military jargon calls them, scores of soldiers out in the desert saw only glowing blobs in their scopes that they misjudged as enemy contacts, but were in reality elements of their own forces.

This brings us to the subject of what we saw as opposed to what we didn't. There is little or no publicly available photographic documentation of actual Gulf War fighting. In fact, there is virtually nothing in print either. Among the few prose glimpses that did emerge during the hundred combat hours of the Gulf War was one in the form of an article by *Los Angeles Times* reporter John Balzar concerning a videotape from an Apache helicopter's gun camera on a night mission against Iraqi bunkers. Balzar's report graphically described how the Iraqis were blown to bits by 30 millimeter autofire and high explosive rocket salvos by an unseen enemy in the dark of night.

Though the story miraculously made it through military censors, the gun camera video was never seen or heard from again, and no other reports in the mass media of close-up fighting had ever been filed until long after the war had ended. Yet there was literally a mountain of high-quality photographic, video and other visual data that could have been shown to the public, even had news teams with minicams been barred from taping live combat engagements. Yet even this evidence, which came from videotapes of automatic recorders on weapons systems, was tightly suppressed by military censors.

The only visual record of the Gulf War consists of what the military permitted us to see, and this wasn't the actual face of war, but a sanitized, dumbed-down version that downplayed virtually anything that ran contrary to the official storyline.

Day after day, television viewers were shown gun camera videotape depicting flawless performance of laser-guided bombs penetrating their targets and exploding with spectacular results, such as the famous sequence of a smart bomb going down the airshaft of the building housing the headquarters of Iraqi intelligence in downtown Baghdad. The four-letter words and whooping cheers of the gun crews were also cut out of the audio tracks of the footage so that pilots universally sounded like altar boys instead of airmen pumped up on adrenaline in the midst of battle.

But a vastly greater amount of footage that showed countless bombs missing their targets entirely was also suppressed by military censors. This included taped sequences of the supposedly super-accurate bomb delivery systems of the F-117 Stealth fighter-bomber due to such factors as pilot error, systems malfunctions and unforeseen weather glitches. Another class of footage that was marked as "never to be viewed" by the American public was that which showed hits scored by friendly fire. A third form of censored imagery was anything that even remotely showed death or wounding in combat, as if this sort of thing didn't happen on the modern battlefield!

To an extent, the Pentagon's antipathy to the news media can be understood in the wake of the often one-sided coverage during the war in Vietnam, where the military was all-too-frequently demonized by a hostile press corps. Also, a press corps that at the time of Desert Storm boasted few members who had ever seen combat firsthand, and many who could not seem to display even a rudimentary knowledge of the basic concepts of war (many an M16 rifle was upgraded to "machine gun" status by credulous reporters), understandably antagonized the military.

Nevertheless, never before in this century has U.S. war coverage been so completely stage-managed and overtly propagandistic. America is not a nation of cowards and fully understands the necessity of going to war. Furthermore, U.S. opposition to war, even in the case of Vietnam, was more often based on casualties of U.S. soldiers rather than the fate of enemy troops or even foreign civilian casualties. Not revealing more about the Gulf War was a case of ill-founded over-reaction by both the media and the Pentagon. Americans should have been told far more concerning what was really happening in the Gulf instead of being subjected to a cover-up of sizable proportions.

IMPACT ANALYSIS

The absence of fuller disclosure can and will weaken U.S. resolve to fight a full-blown future war that would inevitably prove longer and bloodier than the Desert Storm campaign.

During the Grenada invasion, for example, protests poured into *Life* magazine over a photo of a Cuban soldier burned to death in a bombing raid. The single photo, tame compared to the weekly photospreads of the Vietnam era, let alone World War II, garnered angry protests from shocked readers.

Imagine the horror of the twenty-first century's home front on viewing unsanitized video images of war, an inevitability once any given war continues for any appreciable length of time in the electronic age. The results could be, as Charlie Chan liked to say, most unfortunate.

V 🧩

POW/MIA Cover-ups

When most of us today hear or read the acronyms POW and MIA we immediately think of Vietnam and the controversy surrounding persistent rumors of American prisoners of war still held in prison camps in Indochina. Not many of us think of the Korean War, and fewer, if any, mentally flash on World War II—unless it's maybe to picture U.S. GIs held in German or Japanese prison camps.

I'd venture to guess that only rarely in this last connection would the terms POW or MIA evoke thoughts of soldiers officially declared killed or missing in action, but actually held prisoner in secret places.

After all, our side won the Second World War, and all our fighting forces came home, to victory parades down the main streets of American towns and cities. They returned to start new lives, and all were accounted for. Even soldiers who were captured by the enemy eventually were released after the fighting stopped.

Or were they?

No military force in the history of warfare has ever considered its rank and file as anything except totally expendable. Forget the public relations and the slick TV advertisements for our all-volunteer army.

When a soldier joins up, he or she signs away most of the rights that U.S. civilians are constitutionally guaranteed. The soldier becomes a tool of military commanders, in much the same sense that a rifle or a tank is the tool of the soldier in combat. This assessment sounds harsh, and it is harsh, but it's also reality, and a principle as old as war itself that every soldier gets to know sooner or later. Downed Gulf War pilots, who'd been assured that rescue teams would make every effort to extract them but found out differently once behind enemy lines, are among the latest to learn this fact.

This principle extends not only to combat risks, but includes political accountability as well. A soldier can be sacrificed to the expediency of military operations, but can also be sacrificed to the exigencies of political circumstances. This means that when the war is over and the peace is declared, those left behind may become embarrassments and liabilities and considered impediments to the prevailing postwar order.

As the Gulf War has once again demonstrated, the traditional reaction of military brass is to cover up and stonewall when some of the dirtier secrets natural to the waging of any war are brought to light. The stonewalling surrounding the illness that has come to be known as Gulf War Syndrome, for example, demonstrates that little has changed in this regard.

In past wars, there was little challenging of official pronouncements on the issue of kin missing in action. When a family received notification that a member was killed or had gone missing in combat, it usually wasn't questioned. In earlier eras, many official matters were rarely questioned.

But things have obviously changed. More than thirty years since the end of the war in Indochina the controversy surrounding Vietnam POW/MIAs is still current. One of the consequences of this ongoing polemic has been new questions concerning the fate of captured U.S. servicemen in previous wars America has fought.

In the closing months of World War II the Allied armies of the East and West were rapidly drawing a noose tight around the fading German Reich.

It was a race to see who would get to Berlin first, and the Soviets were determined not to lose any ground to the Americans and the British, who they were planning to double-cross after the war anyway. Soviet despot Joseph Stalin's strategy called for grabbing as much territory as possible before a cease-fire was declared, and afterward refusing to budge. Stalin surmised that once the war was over, the West would lose its stomach for renewed fighting. The shrewd Soviet dictator wasn't far from wrong.

As the Soviets triumphantly marched across German-held territory in Eastern Europe, grinding up Nazi troops in their path like Wiener schnitzel, they acquired thousands of German prisoners. The usual fate of these luckless captives was to be taken back to mother Russia on forced death marches that would slowly and painfully kill most of them through starvation, disease and exposure to the elements. Out of thousands of captured Wehrmacht and SS troops, only a few hundred were to survive the ordeal of being Ivan's "guests."

So much for Nazi POWs, and many may say all well and good—who gives a damn? But there is another facet to the story, one which concerns U.S. prisoners of war who were also scooped up by the advancing Soviet forces.

These American GIs had been formerly captured by German troops and shipped off to POW camps in the Nazi-held "eastern territories" of Poland, Czechoslovakia and the Balkan republics by their captors. To these prisoners, the approaching Soviet troops were allies and therefore greeted as liberators. At least that's how the Americans regarded them at first blush.

The Soviets looked at the situation somewhat differently, though. As stated, Stalin's postwar ambitions called for grabbing bearish armfuls of Eastern Europe to establish Soviet satellite republics. The Soviet dictator knew that the more leverage he could exert to make the West back down in the face of Soviet intransigence, the better. Holding hundreds of American prisoners as bargaining chips was considered by Stalin and his number two man, Lavrenti Beria, to be one effective way of guaranteeing that the West played ball.

In other cases, in which some GIs possessed specialized technical knowledge that was of value to various postwar Soviet weapons programs, their participation in research was forced by their captors. As a result of this policy, the "liberated" American POWs soon found themselves prisoners for the second time in a row, only now in the hands of their supposed Soviet "allies."

Since these prisoners were of more value to Soviet postwar aims alive than dead, they were given far better treatment than the captured Germans were afforded. Instead of being marched into Russia on foot, they were put onboard long lines of boxcars and shipped by rail to detention camps in Siberia and the Ukraine.

These secret camps made up a "Gulag Archipelago" that was separate from the gulag—or string of secret camps—warehousing native Soviet political prisoners. To the rest of the world the U.S. POWs held in Soviet captivity were either dead or missing in action.

Actually the word "secret," when applied to the camps, isn't completely accurate, since U.S. intelligence agencies, including the Defense Intelligence Agency (DIA), knew all about the prisoners' existence from the get-go. Over the course of time, and despite a decades-long policy of outright denial by the U.S. government, compelling evidence has emerged in support of the Soviet Union having held American prisoners after World War II and the Korean War.

Some of this evidence has come in the form of declassified KGB and GRU (Soviet military intelligence) documents. These began to be released after the breakup of the Soviet Union in the late 1980s. Adding to the body of evidence have been admissions by Moscow that U.S. prisoners of war had been warehoused by the Soviets in secret camps inside Russia.

Other documents concerning the whereabouts of the imprisoned U.S. troops have come from the U.S. Department of Defense. Records released under the Freedom of Information Act, some of these dating back to 1946, reveal that the U.S. government brought down a curtain of cover-up about the World War II MIAs just as Stalin was lowering the Iron Curtain on the USSR.

The U.S. files, in the form of hundreds of records of sightings and eyewitness reports, manifest the clear knowledge that former GIs were being held inside Russia. Even today, full disclosure of the many more files concerning the sad fate of World War II MIAs imprisoned in Russia has been blocked by the Pentagon, which claims that disclosure would somehow compromise "national security" more than a half century after the fact.

Apart from these confirmations, there are accounts from credible eyewitnesses, such as retired General Orval A. Anderson, an operations officer who was formerly attached to the Eighth Air Force in Europe during the Second World War. According to Anderson, it was "common knowledge" that U.S. Army Air Corps personnel being held prisoner in German POW camps in Poland were taken by the Soviets and never returned. Anderson stated that Allied officers "pleaded with [General George C.] Marshall to fly in, take over the prisons and take people out."

Marshall vetoed these proposals, as his successors a few decades later vetoed similar ones made after the fall of Vietnam, and any officer who pressed the issue was in danger of being transferred out of Europe. "We were close to open revolt over the situation," Anderson said, and the military leaders of the United States and Britain were determined to break up a possible mutiny before it started.

At about the same time, on the diplomatic front, W. Averell Harriman, U.S. Ambassador to Moscow from 1944 to 1945, recognized that an international crisis was brewing in Stalin's retention of thousands of U.S., Canadian and British POWs as bargaining chips against Allied moves against entrenched communist positions in Eastern Europe.

Although Harriman urged a hard diplomatic and political line to be taken in lobbying for the release of all POWs, the Roosevelt administration overruled him, and the Truman administration that followed perpetuated this policy.

Weary of the hot war and embarking on the cold war, the U.S. and Britain were not about to take the military option to free Stalin's illegally held prisoners. Nor could they play the communist leader's drawn-out negotiating games in which he tried to milk the West out of concession after concession in money and other forms of foreign aid.

Tiring of the game, most remaining POWs were simply written off by their governments, and a cover-up put in place that remains in effect to the present day.

History in the treatment of U.S. POWs repeated itself in the wake of the Korean War, which followed close on the heels of World War II. In this case, General Douglas MacArthur's retreat to cease-fire lines behind the thirty-eighth parallel resulted in thousands of American GIs scooped up and taken prisoner by advancing Chinese communist troops.

MacArthur's seaborne invasion of North Korea by way of the coastal city of Inchon had at first proven a brilliant tactical stroke. But the hard-charging general had underestimated the enemy and pushed too far too quickly. In the end, the U.S. was forced to accept a negotiated peace settlement instead of the all-out victory that appeared so tantalizingly close soon after the invasion commenced.

From Korea, captured GIs were sent to China where, by all accounts, a sinister refinement of the secret Russian POW camp system was soon established by their Maoist captors. In these hidden Chinese POW camps, certain prisoners deemed useful to the communists were culled out from the general population. These were placed in an entirely separate prison system, one that had a no-return policy.

The POWs sent to these special camps would never see the outside world again, no matter what happened. While a second POW coverup descended on the American public, U.S. GIs languished in secret camps in China, Siberia and North Korea from which they would never escape to the outside world.

The reasons why communists continued to hold these prisoners after the Korean War, which ended in 1953, is largely the same as those that underlay Stalin's earlier strategy, and are in fact closely based upon them.

These POWs of the early phase of the Cold War served the same roles as economic and political bargaining chips, sources of technical knowledge, and as a pool of slave labor that World War II's MIAs had done. And, just as had been the case before, the United States permitted negotiation efforts to slip and peter out after some initial concessions were made and a few prisoners were released.

But this time, not everyone blandly accepted the assurances that all U.S. servicemen had returned home after the end of the Korean War. President Dwight D. Eisenhower began to face a landslide of protest, in the form of letter blitzes and demonstrations in front of the White House, from the relatives of GIs who had not returned.

There were also calls for military action to be taken to force the release of imprisoned soldiers. The Joint Chiefs of Staff readied a plan for a blockade of China by sea and air, but this was vetoed by Eisenhower who feared an escalation of already high cold war tensions, and who typically preferred to back off from international confrontations rather than take aggressive action during the term of his presidency.

Of course, in Ike's defense, such a move would have represented an application of military force that was more drastic than anything that had been undertaken since World War II, even at the height of the Korean War. And by the early fifties, the Soviets already possessed nuclear weapons and a bomber fleet that could reach clear across Europe. Ike, perhaps justifiably, feared that going too far could trigger a nuclear war, and that military reprisals represented a clear case of going too far.

Yet by 1955, two years after the Korean War's end, there were reliable intelligence reports that reached Eisenhower identifying up to a thousand American prisoners of war in the hands of the Soviets, POWs that were being incarcerated in remote Siberian camps.

One report, still officially classified, was made to Eisenhower by Colonel Philip Corso (whose revelations about UFOs will be dealt with in a coming chapter), who tacitly acknowledged the fact that cold war realities meant that the United States had zero options to get back its POWs.

Corso had written: "I recommended that the report not be made public because the POWs should be given up for being dead since we knew the Soviets would never relinquish them. Out of concern for the POWs' families, the President agreed."

Others shared this view. A 1955 report titled *Recovery of Unrepatriated Prisoners of War*, compiled by the Pentagon's Defense Advisory Committee on Prisoners of War, stated a number of sobering conclusions.

It argued that the United States could not realistically use overwhelming military force against the three communist countries that were holding the POWs. Even if military force were employed, more war prisoners would die in the event than would be saved. It would also pose the distinct threat of triggering a nuclear war between the superpowers.

As far as the POWs went, the report concluded, "We have been unable, under existing national policy considerations, to bring about an accounting by the Commies." The POWs would stay where they were and the curtain of secrecy would be kept in place about their true whereabouts in enemy hands for many years to come.

These grim conclusions, and the sobering realization that the United States had twice in the course of a single decade been faced with global adversaries who had held onto captured GIs with the deliberate aim of using them as bargaining chips to gain political leverage and economic aid, became part of a major turning point in American military policy.

The Pentagon began to cast its gaze forward to the kinds of wars that America might have to fight in the future, and began to plan accordingly. Before, POW issues had been handled on an ad hoc basis, but in the future there would be a secret agenda that would dictate the way we responded to similar POW blackmail attempts by the next set of adversaries the nation faced.

This secret agenda would be part of a new policy on the fighting of what was termed "limited war" by Pentagon studies of the 1950s. These studies were taking note of a potential battleground for American troops in the coming decade—a remote, impoverished and unimportant jungle-covered country called French Indochina, less frequently known by the name its people had christened their land—*Vietnam.*

While the United States was occupied in Korea, the French were embroiled in their own war in Vietnam. The former French colony, like so many other former satrapies of Europe's Great Powers in the postwar years, was struggling to break free of its erstwhile colonial masters. Also, like many other nations in what would soon come to be called the Third World, communism was the political system of choice for Vietnam's intellectual elite, which equated capitalism with the gunboat diplomacy and triangular trade systems that had been imposed on their country by alien conquerors.

The United States was subsidizing the war efforts of the French, but had also indirectly subsidized the North Vietnamese, since massive quantities of weapons, ammunition and military vehicles that had been captured by the Red Chinese and North Koreans during U.S. involvement in Korea, had been shipped south for use by Ho Chi Minh's insurrectionist forces during the civil war in Vietnam.

With the French losing the Indochina war, and often losing badly, there was significant political pressure for the United States to move in and take over the fighting should the French pull out. Vietnam was seen by foreign policy analysts in the White House and elsewhere as the linchpin of Southeast Asia. If it fell to the communists, other former Great Power colonies and sources of natural wealth in vital strategic materials, such as Malaysia, Singapore, Thailand and Burma, to name but a few, might also fall to the encroaching communist hordes.

When the French ultimately did withdraw from Vietnam after the debacle at Dien Bien Phu, America was ready to step in and take over the fight. But unlike the case with Korea, the Pentagon had already formulated a secret plan for the prosecution of that war, which was in part determined by the secret history of the POW/MIAs from World War II and Korea.

As the 1955 Defense Advisory Committee report stated, "If we are 'at war,' cold, hot or otherwise, casualties and losses must be expected and perhaps we must learn to live with this type of thing. If we are in for fifty years of peripheral 'fire fights' we may be forced to adopt a rather cynical attitude on this for political reasons."

The implication was clear: in Vietnam the United States would commit itself to a war-fighting strategy that enshrined the diametrical opposite of the philosophy that had guided it in the past. The next war would be fought with cold-blooded pragmatism and few of the lofty ideals that had underlain America's entrance into two previous world wars and one four-year "police action." If the enemy chose to fight dirty—and the experience of the French showed that he almost surely *would* fight dirty—then we would respond in kind.

To use a phrase from another white paper on future war from that era, America would adopt a "human chess game" approach to the new limited wars that were to engage us in the future. The phrase came from an alleged secret 1957 study prepared for the Department of Defense and which was to serve as a blueprint for these new and vicious "limited wars."

The author of the study was said to be a young Ph.D. making a name for himself in political circles—Henry Kissinger. The report (which an older Kissinger later denied having ever written at all), called for the adoption of a policy guided mainly by pragmatism. The report has been labeled "cynical," but at the same time it can be argued that it was grounded on a set of realities that might be harsh, but did in fact exist.

Among the study's conclusions was that the United States could no longer afford to permit its enemies to use American prisoners of war as bargaining chips and leveraging tools to force concessions from the United States. Such a situation was tantamount to America winning the war but losing the peace.

Moreover, the very concept of limited war bespeaks a political rather than a military solution to hostilities. Since the United States would not aim for total control of the enemy's territory but merely to do enough damage to force the other side to the bargaining table (shades of Desert Storm), there would be no viable military option to guarantee the safe return of war prisoners. This meant that when future enemies claimed they had no more prisoners, America's response would be to shrug and pass it off as part of the price paid for victory.

This seems to be exactly what has happened in the case of American prisoners in Vietnam who have never been acceptably accounted for. Despite strong evidence to suggest that American prisoners have been held in Vietnam, and even the Soviet Union, since well after the fall of Saigon in April 1975 and the American pull-out from Indochina, the official government line is that no U.S. POWs remain unaccounted for. Yet the POW sightings continue and, even after almost twenty-five years, many of them are considered highly credible.

A semiofficial effort to free prisoners sighted in a camp in Laos was undertaken in 1982. Known as Operation Lazarus, the effort was financed in part by Ross Perot and run by former Special Forces Major Bo Gritz. Lazarus, which involved the insertion of a covert rescue force of mercenaries into Laos, was a latter-day avatar of the aborted Operation Velvet Hammer, a mission to free Laotian captives near the end of the Indochina war that was scrubbed at the eleventh hour.

Although the Lazarus rescue team infiltrated successfully into the Laotian jungle, it ultimately became entangled in enemy spoiling attacks and was beset with a growing uncertainty of whether there were any prisoners there to rescue after all. In the end, the mission failed. Gritz, among others, has claimed that the CIA tipped off the Laotians to forestall the possibility of any Americans emerging from their long imprisonment to reveal embarrassing secrets the agency would prefer kept forgotten.

IMPACT ANALYSIS

Prisoners of war in the hands of unscrupulous enemies have put America in a double bind, one that hurts the country whichever way it turns. As long as the cover-up stays secret, it tends to have some political justification. Once the secret is out, though, the knowledge of such a policy can undermine support on the home front. I believe that this is one of the issues that contributed to the military's nervousness about telling the truth concerning Desert Storm. But the next war that America fights may not go so smoothly—by covering up, the Pentagon may have laid the groundwork for a future "Vietnam syndrome" that, fueled by skepticism and the speed of electronic media, sets in much more rapidly than the "classic edition."

VI

Weird Science

If you've been moved by the urge to line your ball cap with aluminum foil, hear voices in your head telling you to perform strange and unnatural acts or remember things that never happened (at least to you), then the good news is you might not be crazy. The bad news is that it might be the CIA that's either programming your mind like a VCR or beaming psychotronic weapons emissions at your think gland for sinister purposes.

In fact, some conspiracy theorists hold that we're all just human TV dinners doing a slow burn in a global microwave oven, and that malevolent forces of various kinds have already been bombarding the planet with rays of doom for many years. The thought controllers, they say, have perfected insidious technologies for programming the human brain, warping the human mind and twisting the human psyche like modeling clay in the hands of a nursery-school Picasso.

Their ultimate aim is said to be the spread of mass paranoia, psychic depression and almost hallucinatory madness that will render us all incapable of resisting the coming takeover by a one-world government. I wonder—could Marilyn Manson and Rob Zombie be a part of all this?

Nor is any corner of the time-space continuum safe from the malicious tampering of clandestine science. Forays into the realms of future time as well as the manipulation of the long-dead past are all part of the bizarre wizardry of oddball experimenters.

Not content to project voices into the heads of their hapless victims, these clandestine Karloffs have even devised means of invading our very dreams, and the astral selves of psychic warriors routinely ply the ether as disembodied James Bonds, spying and sneaking and skulking and scanning where no walls can hinder them.

Even the dreaded scourge of AIDS is said by many to have been the result of efforts to create a biological weapon capable of selectively wiping out undesirable segments of the population. On the other side of the coin, the true cure for AIDS is said to be in the possession of those same hidden manipulators, protecting a select few against the ravages of the dreaded disease while permitting them to engage in debauched orgies at the taxpayers' expense that would make a Nero blush with embarrassment.

Let's not forget the mind-disruption vans that, disguised as snack food delivery trucks and other commonly encountered vehicles, drive around and beam the vibes of havoc at selected enemies of the state that can cause death in fifteen minutes (or so it's said).

In fact, you could probably make a case that even writers of books about conspiracy could be programmed by distant manipulators to use mocking language about what is really a deadly threat and make light of a serious matter. This is not to imply for a second that klepton ixca mistxo blorg noctrin iutios I consider myself uilos tyousn mfllsgs glupxx, so you can be sure this book's not not one one of them of them of of them them!

Before delving into the world of spooky science, here follows a brief primer on one of the potentates of applied physics, Nikola Tesla. It's important to know a bit about the naturalized Czech electrical genius because his name crops up again and again in this area.

Though foreign-born, Nikola Tesla spent most of his career in the United States until his death in the 1940s. Tesla, who was a contemporary of such other scientific notables as Albert Einstein and Thomas A. Edison, figured in a number of initiatives both civilian and military that were to shape the course of twentieth-century American life for decades to come.

One of the most profound of these endeavors led to the great debate between the virtues of alternating current (AC) power as opposed to direct current (DC) power that prevailed at the turn of the century. By 1911 Europe's major cities, including Paris and London, had already traded in their nineteenth-century gaslights for modern electrical public street lighting. America was about to follow their lead, but not before a heated debate over standards that potentially held untold millions of dollars at stake was settled.

Thomas Edison, backed by the General Electric company, championed alternating current as the source of America's imminent electrification program. Tesla, who represented Westinghouse, pushed for direct current, which was—and still is—the type of current used throughout most of Europe.

Both forms of electrical power had advantages and disadvantages. Alternating current could be transmitted across greater distances than direct current, which meant fewer power stations needed to be built. On the other hand, direct current, which required more numerous power stations, was considered safer.

A fierce battle was waged between the two camps, but in the end General Electric won, giving the United States alternating current and contributing to Tesla's slide into poverty that ended in a cheap hotel on Manhattan's west side, near the street on the north end of midtown's Bryant Park that today bears his name.

Tesla was into more than just "current" events, though. A great deal more. In fact, there was very little concerning the electromagnetic spectrum that Mr. T. did not investigate or experiment with in some way, shape or form. Nor were Tesla's interests solely confined to the realm of so-called "pure" science, but for the most part all had real-world applications.

The scale of Tesla's known work encompasses an immense assortment of revolutionary and exotic energy devices. Particle beam weapons, wireless energy transmission machines, lasers and time travel schemes are all part of his prodigious output. It should be added that the full extent of Tesla's work is still not publicly known, since all his papers were confiscated by the U.S. government upon Tesla's death, over the protests of the executors of his estate, and never fully made public.

It is held as an article of faith by conspiracy theorists that the fruits of Tesla's strange genius have been harvested by clandestine scientific programs in the service of covert weapons applications design. Tesla tech is said to have been the basis for much of Strategic Defense Initiative technology and many other spook science projects, including radiotelemetric mind control weaponry.

Possibly the most famous, or infamous, projects in conspiracy lore based on Tesla technology are two allegedly secret programs, which, though separated by forty years and hundreds of miles, are nonetheless said to be linked together in a variety of extremely weird ways. This complex of covert convergence is constituted by the so-called Philadelphia Experiment (PX) and the Montauk Project.

The Philadelphia Experiment is said to have begun with an attempt, following Pearl Harbor, by the U.S. Navy to shroud or Trekkishly "cloak" its warships with a stealthy energy field rendering them invisible, either to radar or optical viewing or to both simultaneously.

The basis for the experiment is said to have been Einstein's unified field theory, which was an attempt by Albert Einstein to link magnetic and gravitational forces in the same way that his nuclear theory had demonstrated the linkage between energy and mass.

The latter, which produced the now-famous equation $E=mc^2$, provided the key to the nuclear physics underlying the development of the atomic bomb. As to the unified field theory, it could theoretically have held the key to space warping, time travel, antigravity propulsion systems, teleportation and a host of other applications, such as those very same strange inventions that Tesla was dreaming up in New York.

While Einstein withdrew his unified field theory as incomplete and officially never solved it, there are those who believe this to be untrue, arguing that like Tesla's confiscated papers, the complete theory became the basis for covert scientific experimentation by the U.S. government. They argue that the occurrence of the Philadelphia Experiment confirms the existence of a completed unified field theory by Einstein.

As with virtually everything else concerning the PX, accounts of when, where and by what means it took place tend to differ. The test bed for the experiment is said to have been the U.S.S. *Eldridge,* a destroyer–escort vessel that, at the time of the experiment, was newly commissioned for active service. Some accounts place the time and date of the test at July 2, 1943, others at October 28, 1943, while still others claim there were two tests, one taking place on each date.

Similarly, there is disagreement concerning the exact

nature of the technological means used to perform the experiment. At one end of the spectrum, the USN claims that nothing more exotic than the degaussing (or demagnetizing) of the *Eldridge*'s hull to protect the ship against magnetically triggered sea mines was being carried out. At the other, an assortment of thermal, electromagnetic and gravitational generating systems built into the *Eldridge* have also been proposed.

The most common view on this subject is that the Eldridge was equipped with four massive Tesla coils, two located on its port and two on its starboard hulls. The coils, wound with miles and miles of wire, and acting as gargantuan magnetic field generators, were powered by two large electrical generators situated where the ship's main guns would normally have been located. The power from these generators was fed through the coils to generate oscillating magnetic field pulses that were controlled by a tube-driven processor system, that is, a primitive computer system onboard the ship.

The resulting rotational force field was said to have had an instantaneous warping effect on the local space-time continuum surrounding the *Eldridge*.

Whether or not the one- or two-test version of the experiment is to be believed, the results are said to have exceeded all expectations. The ship was enveloped in a greenish haze, then disappeared entirely, some say after an accompanying flash of brilliant blue light. Seconds later it rematerialized at Norfolk Harbor, some fifteen miles away. In a heartbeat, the *Eldridge* next vanished from Norfolk and was back in Philadelphia harbor.

When naval investigators boarded the ship, they were supposed to have been greeted with an even more astonishing sight: all members of the *Eldridge*'s crew had been transformed in bizarre and frightening ways. Some had simply gone insane. Others were even more profoundly altered. Some of these crewmen had completely lost their material forms. They flickered in and out of reality, then vanished completely. Other sailors were found embedded in the railings of the ship or in the steel deck, while still others could pass unhindered through solid objects.

Even those who had not been physically changed and who later regained their sanity experienced serious aftereffects of the incident. Among these aftereffects was the propensity to suddenly, and permanently, vanish at odd times and places. One crewman is said to have gotten up from the family dinner table and walked through a wall, never to return (talk about eating and running). Another, it is claimed, spontaneously dematerialized during a fistfight with another man, in front of several witnesses, a trick Roberto Duran could have probably used a few decades later.

Another PX aftereffect came to be known as "freezing" or "getting stuck." Here, ex-crewmen became incapable of physical movement, speech or any form of interaction with the outside world. These episodes could last anywhere from hours to days to months and often resulted in raving lunacy when the victims unfroze again (this sort of reminds me of being married).

It's also claimed that the laying on of hands by other ex-crewmen helped some of the initial freezing victims, until one consoling practitioner of this Bizarro World therapeutic touch spontaneously burst into unquenchable flames and burned for eighteen days, despite every effort to put out the fire. After this, laying on of hands was discontinued (though I wonder if they ever tried asbestos potholders like mom used to have in the kitchen).

As if all this weren't weird enough, it gets weirder still. Supposedly the *Eldridge* and its crew were not merely teleported a few miles away but were also transported forty years into the future, to the year 1983.

There, those who were not fused to metal, drooling and gibbering like chimps or beaming in and out of existence, jumped overboard into what they thought was Philadelphia Harbor. Except it was the waters of Long Island Sound they hit, right off the coast of Montauk, Long Island, to be exact.

Swimming ashore, they found (to them) futuristic-looking soldiers outfitted in camouflage fatigues and packing M16 rifles who conducted them into an underground base where a grizzled old scientist was waiting for them. They'd been expected, he told them; expected for a long time. The scientist was none other than John von Neumann, director of the original Philadelphia Experiment back in '43, who had been waiting forty years for the time travelers' arrival.

Von Neumann (now more like "von Oldman") ordered the time-warped sailors back on the *Eldridge* because the experiment had created a rift in the fabric of space and time that might ultimately cause a chain re-action of sorts and engulf the entire planet in a super time warp that would make us all part of a *Flintstones* episode. Von Neumann apparently didn't bother telling his guests that they would get all messed up when they chrono-jumped back to the past. But he being a mad-scientist type, this omission probably isn't that surpris-ing.

(In my opinion, he could have at least said, "Listen, guys. Some of you will feel a little headachy when you get back, but not to worry. Just take two aspirin and call me in forty years.") (Okay, bad joke, but they can't all be zingers, now, can they?)

Moreover, due to certain periodic cyclical variations in the earth's magnetic field, the monkeying around with gravitational forces by the navy had allegedly opened up a time tunnel linking Philadelphia in 1943 with Long Island in 1983. (Does the fact that the Vil-lage People did the song "In the Navy" around that time have anything to do with this?)

On top of everything else, aliens from the star Zeta Reticuli had set up the whole weird shebang, sublim-inally programming naval minds to conduct the Phil-adelphia Experiment at the exact date during which it took place in order to create a cosmic resonance for their own nefarious ends. (For all I know, aliens also created the Long Island Expressway, which is obvi-ously an insidious plan to thwart all attempts at earth-ling automotive travel.) (Okay, I'll cut it out already.)

By 1983, thanks to alien intervention, a host of strange covert science experiments was being carried out at the secret Montauk base. These included time travel and the creation of evil mind beings like the "Id" creature from the B-movie classic *Forbidden Planet*, which, in my case, fostered certain Freudian fantasies about the female star instead of goose bumps over the monster. (Not that this has anything to do with anything.) (I lied, I won't cut it out!)

Actually, I'm not surprised to hear about strange warps out on Long Island, since I've always felt L.I. was an evil place. The evidence? I know a lot of literary agents who live out on Long Island, for one thing.

Then, there's the Long Island Railroad, which a pistol-packing whacko once turned into a shooting gallery one rush-hour evening. Then there was the case of the "Long Island Lolita." Then there's the alleged shoot-down of TWA flight 800 near Montauk Air Force Base, which some claim to have been the result of a botched heat-seeking nuclear missile test.

Also, I have a strange memory of once taking the train onto Long Island, getting off, walking around, then coming back to where I started. But I can't remember why or when. Since I would never consciously set foot on Long Island, I can only surmise that aliens must have taken over my brain and made me go there for some reason I'd rather not contemplate.

Apart from its connection to the Philadelphia Experiment, the Montauk Project also figures as a clandestine research center with tie-lines to another preoccupation with conspiracy theorists—mind control and biotelemetric weaponry.

At Montauk's secret underground base, experiments in the linkage of computers to human minds were supposedly carried out on a regular basis. Von Neumann is said to have believed that the human mind possessed unlimited power. When brain waves were properly amplified and modulated by computers, these energies could generate matter, time vortexes and even make human bodies explode, as depicted at the conclusion of the Brian De Palma feature film *The Fury,* which is claimed by some to have been based on von Neumann's work.

This is only one aspect of the clandestine experimentation on mind control and weaponry that's supposedly being carried out by secret governmental agencies. Von Neumann's just-cited work sounds like a fringe fantasy and probably is a fringe fantasy, but there are more believable reports of clandestine efforts to attack, control and mobilize the forces of the human mind as a target and tool of modern warfare.

Some of these, such as aspects of the secret MK-ULTRA project, have been documented, while others, which bear up somewhat better under scrutiny than the Philadelphia Experiment story, but haven't left an extensive paper trail, cannot be dismissed out of hand.

MK-ULTRA, named at least in part for Millbrook mansion, which was a setting for many experiments connected with the project, was concerned with exploring the use of an estimated 149 chemical agents in an attempt to build an arsenal of mind control weapons.

Psychoactive drugs of all description were experimented with on witting and unwitting test subjects, civilian and military alike, toward perfecting substances that would run the gamut from incapacitating soldiers on the battlefield to creating instant human puppets.

Sparked by revelations concerning psychological and chemical programming ("brainwashing") of U.S. prisoners of war by the Japanese and later by the Red Chinese and North Koreans, and aware that the Soviets were conducting experimentation along these same lines themselves, U.S. war planners and intelligence cadres saw themselves in a race to close the "mind gap" along with the "missile gap" and other "gaps" existing between the West and East.

As it turned out, Lysergic Acid Diethylamide-25 (LSD) was ultimately considered to be the best candidate for an effective chemical warfare and mind control agent. LSD had been synthesized in the early 1940s by the now-celebrated Albert Hofmann, a chemist working for the Swiss pharmaceutical firm Sandoz. The intense sensory hallucinations produced by the action of LSD on the human brain and nervous system seemed to betoken great promise for the hoped-for wonder drug of warfare.

At Millbrook, a team of government-sponsored researchers, including Richard Alpert, who later became better known as the guru Ram Dass, engaged in bouts of round-the-clock acid tripping. Despite some bad trips, the researchers' collective experience was largely a positive one. But then again, they were surrounded with cool paintings, Persian rugs, tanks full of exotic tropical fish and a sense of professional if not spiritual comradeship.

Other MK-ULTRA test subjects didn't fare as well, especially unwitting subjects who were secretly dosed with CIA acid and never told that they were being sent into the lysergic void as part of a hush-hush military experiment.

Unaware of what was happening to them, some of these subjects began to freak out and then lapsed into psychotic or catatonic states, many of them permanent. Even several subjects who had recovered from their bad trips were never the same again.

Albert Hofmann's Swiss freak-out juice had French-fried their neurons, dendrites, synapses and other mental hardware connections, giving them acid flashbacks and other symptoms all too familiar to those involved with the drug counterculture of the '60s, itself in part a legacy of covert LSD experimentation.

By the mid-sixties it had become apparent that neither LSD nor any other drug in the covert pharmacopeia was likely to create instant Manchurian candidates for the CIA or induce a regiment of Red Chinese troops to spontaneously drop their AK-47s and gather posies instead.

Lucy might have been in the sky with diamonds as far as the Beatles went, but around the time *Sgt. Pepper's Lonely Hearts Club Band* was released—along with Tim Leary setting the stage for popular civilian experimentation with acid—the U.S. government was largely out of the drug experimentation business, at least as far as the paper trail goes.

Nonetheless, conspiracy theorists claim that MK-ULTRA research continued, albeit shifting its focus to electromagnetic projection, bio-implantation of microminiature control mechanisms and psychological conditioning as a means of mind control.

If the conspiracy theorists are to be believed, MK-ULTRA is with us to the present day, perfecting new and better methods of mental programming in the service of the coming New World Order. What's more, clandestine manipulators are supposedly using these techniques to program us at this very moment.

As far as addictive drugs go, the conspiraholics say that they've been made available on the street by clandestine forces as part of a massive campaign of total control leading to the enslavement of mankind.

Heavy stuff, but how much of it is wack? If the boldness of certain claims by outspoken conspiracy theorists were a criteria for credibility, then the stories would be highly credible.

Then again, Chicken Little was also highly outspoken, yet the sky never did fall in, now did it? On the other hand, there have been some scraps of hard evidence that have been reported by reputable sources over the years that merit consideration.

In 1970, a book called *Psychic Discoveries Behind the Iron Curtain* appeared that made convincing claims concerning Soviet research into the human mind as both a target and weapon. This sparked a new wave of research by the Department of Defense along avenues previously taken by MK-ULTRA research of the fifties and sixties.

During this period, Polish-born intellectual Zbigniew Brzezinski, who was later to become national security advisor during the Carter administration, wrote of the possibility of using directed energy projection mechanisms as means of affecting the functioning of the human brain in target populations.

Not long thereafter, experimenters at applied physics laboratories conducting research for the Defense Advance Research Projects Agency (DARPA) allegedly discovered that so-called microwave audiograms—the microwave analog of sound waves—could be detected by the human nervous system and experienced as auditory signals. That is, voices could be beamed directly into your noggin.

Apart from revelations contained in another influential book on mind control weaponry, *Mind Wars*, by Ronald Macrae, published in 1984, and documentation of research grants for work that appear to be connected with energy-induced mind manipulation and programming, there is not an overabundance of evidence, and certainly no smoking gun.

The bulk of the "evidence" is purely anecdotal, coming from the supposed victims of government mind control programs whose stories often seem farfetched, to put it mildly.

Still, it should be borne in mind that some of the evidence concerning what the ratzis did in places like Auschwitz and Buchenwald is also "soft" or anecdotal, yet no rational person can doubt it all did in fact happen, although I'm not trying to make a comparison between the two cases.

The claims surrounding a microwave energy project known as HAARP as a tool of mass mind manipulation will be mentioned in a later chapter. In a similar vein, conspiracy theorists claim that video footage of microwave antennas pointing at the Branch Davidian compound in Waco, Texas, during the February 1993 siege by the ATF, offers proof of energy weapons being used against the cult, specifically to beam subliminal commands at them to commit mass suicide.

Other allegations concern Monarch, a subprogram of MK-ULTRA that supposedly uses programming techniques to induce multiple personality disorder in its subjects and create a legion of sex slaves and robotic killers in the service of a depraved political elite. This is said to have included George Bush, Ronald Reagan and Bill Clinton, among others (now, Bush and Reagan I can understand, but why would anybody accuse Bill Clinton of being a sex fiend? Ridiculous!).

The declared "trauma of choice" used in Monarch to instill and maintain the mind control effect is claimed to take the form of pseudo–alien abduction scenarios, and the prevailing view among many conspiracy theorists is that a large percentage of alien abduction claims are really staged by the CIA for the express purpose of creating mind control psychodrama.

This also goes for the tiny, spherical implants that have been reportedly found in the head regions of alien abductees. Far from being products of alien technology, the implants are said to be microminiaturized computer processors that amplify remotely beamed signals that zap the brain using advanced technology methods.

In short, the Control Voice can send you into the Outer Limits anytime it chooses. What's more, astral "watchers" can spy on your every movement, and even influence your thinking, according to some commentators.

According to a controversial book, *Psychic Warrior*, government-sponsored programs in a technique called remote viewing have been underway since the early 1980s. Under various projects using different code names, such as Grill Flame, Center Lane, Gondola Wish and Star Gate, remote viewing was apparently developed into, at the very least, an intelligence-gathering tool by the U.S. military.

Moreover, remote viewing has become something of a New Age craze, with no shortage of instructors ready to teach the specialty to aspiring astral travelers—for the right price in most cases. Some of the claims of remote viewing proponents are simply absurd, but you decide.

A good place to begin a trip into the ether are a number of Web sites on the Internet, some of them sponsored by members of the original Star Gate program, and which purport to be devoted to the study of the genuine, grade-A, U.S. government–tested remote viewing technique.

Just mind you don't fly too close to my space, pilgrim. I be packin' a Glock!

IMPACT ANALYSIS

Scientific discoveries and advances have been kept secret in the interests of "national security" for decades, so cover-up claims concerning even bizarre technologies can't be entirely dismissed. To the extent that such claims are true, suppression of important scientific information that could be used to transform our world for the better hurts more than it helps. If so, more of this data needs to be made public.

VII 🧩

A Wilderness of Mirrors

As the millennium rounds the corner, stories of what the spooks are up to have gotten mega-spooky. To hear conspiracy buffs tell it, secret intelligence networks are behind everything from flying saucers to last year's flu season. To recycle a phrase that former CIA director of counterintelligence James Jesus Angleton "coined" from a line from a T. S. Eliot poem to describe the shadow land of spies, we're all living in a wilderness of mirrors (Yes, I know I used it in the introduction. I guess I must like it. If you don't—doom on you.[1]).

But where does fiction leave off and truth begin? Are secret intelligence networks as powerful and as

---

1. Phonetic spelling of a coarse Vietnamese put-down, FYI.

corrupt—to say nothing of as far-reaching—as conspiracy theorists hold?

Do intelligence organizations truly manipulate us by way of covert plots, clandestine schemes and high-tech devices the way some conspiraholics would have it? What is documented and what is unsupported? And what do we even mean by "intelligence organizations" or "spy networks" or "covert operations" in the first place?

According to the CIA's publication *Factbook on Intelligence,* the Central Intelligence Agency was established in September 1947 as a successor to the Office of Strategic Services (OSS)—which had been disbanded in October of 1945, approximately six months after the end of World War II—and the Central Intelligence Group, created by President Harry S. Truman in January 1946.

Under the National Security Act that established it, the CIA was to be responsible for foreign intelligence collection and covert action only. It was expressly prohibited from conducting domestic intelligence or internal security functions. In short, the CIA could not normally operate within the borders of the United States, but it was given a wide latitude in the types of operations that it could perform outside the sanctuary of American shores.

The OSS, which had been established in June 1942 under the Roosevelt administration, had afforded the

United States a foreign intelligence and covert action capability during the war.

Unlike the CIA, which was established by act of Congress, the OSS was never given complete hegemony over foreign intelligence activities. This jurisdiction it shared with various other intelligence and security organizations, such as the Office of Naval Intelligence (ONI) and even the FBI, which had been conducting operations in Latin America since the 1930s and which, like other outfits competing for the wartime intelligence action, jealously protected its area of operation.

The quick postwar disbandment of the OSS was one of the end results of these jurisdictional clashes, especially with the military, which resented the challenge posed by what the Pentagon saw in the espionage agency as a nascent paramilitary organization run by tweedy civilian spymasters.

OSS leaders were frequently recruited from the ranks of academe and political "brain trusts." They represented a culture that clashed with that of the U.S. military of the era, which carried far less intellectual baggage than the current class of technocrats that lead America's troops (Omar Bradley would have probably needed a dictionary to understand Colin Powell; George Patton would have probably thrown the dictionary at him).

The establishment of the Central Intelligence Agency despite the opposition to and powerful resentment against it in the Pentagon and State Department was an outcome of only one thing. This was the emergence of the cold war, for by 1947 it was apparent that the Soviet Union, led by Joseph Stalin, was a nuclear-armed superstate with aggressively expansionist aims.

At the Tripartite Conference at Potsdam, Germany, held immediately after the war in Europe's end in 1945, Truman, Churchill[2] and Stalin sat down to determine the postwar order that was to follow Germany's military defeat and unconditional surrender.

Of prime importance to the West was the bilateral withdrawal of Allied forces from Eastern Europe. Though Stalin agreed to this, his pledge was not honored by the Soviets, who remained in Poland, Hungary, Czechoslovakia and the Balkans.

Nor was there any will on the part of the West to mobilize in order to force Stalin to honor his commitments. Roosevelt was dead and by this time the world was weary of six years of the bloodiest war in human history. When Churchill pressed for military action to oust the Russians from Eastern Europe, he was voted out of office and replaced by a prime minister with more moderate views. In the United States, Truman also showed a lack of zeal for overt action to roll back the Soviets, preferring political and paramilitary solutions. The age of technocratic compromise had arrived.

In this lay the roots of the cold war and the beginning of a process of escalating tensions between East and West. Along with the buildup of the strategic nuclear arsenals of the superpowers, this environment

---

2. Churchill's soon-to-be successor, Clement R. Attlee, was also present.

gave rise to a bipolar world in which covert action and secret intelligence gained more and more legitimacy as time passed.

By 1949, the Central Intelligence Agency Act was legislated, giving the CIA unprecedented fiscal and operational leeway. The act, which was supplementary to the National Security Act of 1947, not only exempted the CIA from disclosure of how it used its classified budget, but permitted the agency to set up "black budgets" or covert funding channels through other federal agencies.

A three-hundred-dollar toilet seat, sold to the army, or a five-hundred-dollar hammer bought by the navy, for example, could wind up as part of the budget for a CIA black operation staged in Guatemala.[3] The Act gave the CIA not only budgetary secrecy but operational secrecy as well. It exempted the CIA from having to disclose its "organization, functions, names, officials, titles, salaries, or numbers of personnel employed."

In essence, the CIA was not legally accountable to anybody for anything at any time and for any reason. Today, despite congressional oversight as a result of

---

3. I'm not claiming this is the only explanation for exorbitant procurement figures for some items. Fraud by defense contractors and Washington Beltway consultants seems endemic to the system. Sting operations, including the FBI's Illwind, have resulted in the prosecution and imprisonment of major players in defense contracting and the levying of millions of dollars in fines from corporations engaged in defense programs for the Pentagon. This fact does not, however, negate my original premise.

the Church Committee hearings of the 1970s and post–cold war revisions to the 1949 Act, the Central Intelligence Agency continues to operate in a largely unaccountable manner.

But the CIA is not the only major intelligence agency in the so-called "intelligence community" of the United States. There is also the National Security Agency (NSA), the Defense Intelligence Agency (DIA), the intelligence functions of the FBI and State Department, and the intelligence functions of the army, navy, air force, marines, Department of Energy (responsible for nuclear intelligence) and still other, less definable "offices for collection of specialized national foreign intelligence" in existence.

In addition, there are also secret intelligence functions of major police departments across the country, in cities from Los Angeles to New York. Virtually all of these local mini spy agencies enjoy liaison with various intelligence organizations existing on the federal level, including the Central Intelligence Agency itself.

It should be obvious that under the catchall justification of national security, secret intelligence and covert action organizations have proliferated in the United States since the start of the cold war. It should also be obvious that the deliberate lack of effective oversight has created fertile ground for the establishment of private intelligence fiefdoms and the conductance of covert operations that, had they been subjected to the review of the electorate, would not have been deemed in the public interest and would never have been sanctioned.

In light of this, it should come as no surprise that U.S. intelligence services have carried on "cowboy" operations and engaged in other excesses for decades. It would be surprising if they had not, all things considered. What America has done is given a carte blanche license to its intelligence services that no citizen in their right mind would ever give to an elected official or accountable public agency.

If your average lawyer, given power of attorney, is likely to embezzle your life savings on gambling weekends in Vegas or Acapulco, then how much greater is the possibility of a dozen secret networks with alphabet soup names going off the deep end on a global and national level?

Have U.S. intelligence agencies engaged in covert operations that have had negative consequences, even serious ones, for the United States and for the world at large? Without a doubt. Are they part of a far-reaching plot to enslave the minds, bodies and souls of humanity in a New World Order, possibly in conjunction with time-warping aliens, Nazi holdovers and transdimensional mutant geeks, as the fringe conspiracy theorists hold? This I doubt.

But let's take a look at some specific situations and see what's growing in the specimen dish.

"Does the Central Intelligence Agency engage in drug trafficking?" asks the CIA's official *Factbook on Intelligence*.

It answers this question by stating, "No. To the contrary, the Central Intelligence Agency assists the U.S. Government effort to thwart drug trafficking by providing [it with] intelligence information."

That the CIA has chosen to address this question at all points to the frequency with which it has been raised over the years. Unlike the case with many other theories, there is a body of historical and documentary information that supports the contention that elements of U.S. intelligence agencies have been in the drug-dealing business for decades as a source of untraceable cash to fund clandestine operations and as a source of zero-accountable funding.

I stress the word "elements" because I don't believe that a deliberate or concerted covert policy to use drugs to fund operations exists at the level of the office of the CIA director. On the contrary, the very lack of oversight built into the system makes it an ideal environment for ad hoc operations of various kinds, including drug running for cash.

There are several covert drug pipelines, such as the Istanbul-to-Marseilles heroin channel that resulted in the notorious French Connection busts of the early seventies. Another channel is the Golden Triangle–to–West Coast connection that originated in the Shan Hills region of the Laos-Thailand-Vietnam transborder area. A third is the cocaine pipeline that stretches from production and refinement centers in Latin America, up through Mexico and into the U.S. Southwest. A fourth is the Afghanistan-Turkey-Pakistan pipeline that feeds the fruit of the heroin poppy into the former Soviet Union and Eastern Europe.

I'll deal with the Shan as an example, because it has a history with U.S. black ops and because I have some personal familiarity with the region that, to paraphrase the shopworn saying, would force me to kill you if I told you about it.

The involvement of U.S. intelligence assets in the Golden Triangle owes to two principal factors. The first is the ancient practice by the Hmong, Nung and other now-vanishing Montagnard tribes native to the region of cultivating the opium poppy for indigenous medicinal and religious purposes. The cultivation of the opium poppy by these peoples dates back thousands of years to neolithic times.

The second factor has its roots in the special relationship that various influential Americans have had with the Chinese since the days of the treaty ports in the mid-nineteenth century. President Franklin Roosevelt's maternal grandfather, Warren Delano, was among these, and FDR himself had close ties to Generalissimo Chiang Kai-shek, who exercised an iron-fisted military dictatorship over the Chinese until his eventual overthrow by Mao Tse-tung in the late 1930s.

As historian Barbara Tuchman's excellent biography of General "Vinegar Joe" Stillwell makes clear, Chiang was as corrupt a ruler as he was an inept military commander. Stillwell, a capable general who by rights should have been given a field command in Europe, regarded Chiang with undisguised contempt. Chiang's leadership was shored up principally because of his staunch anticommunist stance, a familiar theme in

U.S. relations with Third World despots until fairly recently.

After the communist revolution ousted Chiang and his regime, his ranking generals escaped into Indochina and established power bases there. Since Chiang's generals shared their former leader's anticommunist leanings, and hoped to retake Peking much as the Cubans sought to retake Havana in a later era, they were supported by the Americans and the French, who were also involved in Indochina before and after World War II.

With communist insurgency movements taking hold in Laos, Vietnam and elsewhere, Shan generals were used as surrogate armies in support of Western aims. It was during the United States' involvement in Vietnam that their assistance on the periphery of the fighting was considered worth dealing in heroin to fund.

Poppy fields in the Golden Triangle under the control of the Shan generals yielded raw opium, which was processed into heroin base at factories near the cultivation areas. The base was transported to reprocessing centers in Thailand, such as those in the picturesque border city of Chiang Mai, and then shipped out of Southeast Asia as pure or uncut heroin.

Proceeds from the sale of drugs were used to buy weapons by elements of the CIA, and those weapons—along with clandestine operational funds—were covertly shipped back to the Shan to support the waging of anti-insurgent warfare in Laos, Vietnam, and to a lesser extent, Cambodia and Burma.

It has been claimed by some eyewitnesses that much of the exported heroin of the Vietnam War era was sewn into the bodies of U.S. soldiers killed in action and that the average KIA corpse could hold approximately thirty kilograms of horse once the cadaver's internal organs had been removed.

Strange though such a practice might seem, there is reason to take such charges seriously in light of other eyewitness accounts of covert practices involving those "dusted" in the 'Nam. In cases involving combat fatalities during covert missions, for example, there are credible reports of corpses being kept in cold storage and then flown elsewhere to "die" due to the secrecy of their missions.

Thus, a soldier engaged in America's secret war in Laos during the early 1970s might turn up dead in a car crash in Munich, Germany, where he had "been on leave."

Why was this arcane subterfuge necessary? Among other reasons, because the participation of paramilitary groups based in the Shan was covert and required deniability.

Why did it continue? Because rogue intelligence elements began using drug running as a lucrative source of funding for other covert operations as well. In the cases of those operations conducted on American soil it was especially necessary to have a deniable source of covert funding. You could even say that U.S. intelligence became fiscally addicted to the practice.

This same pattern was followed during the surrogate

warfare in Latin America during the Reagan-Bush years of the 1980s in covert efforts to fund the Contras, led by another group of ousted generals, in this case escaped honchos from Nicaragua.

Here too, the repressive regime of an anticommunist dictator, Anastasio Somóza, was overthrown in a popular uprising, creating a similar fallout of disgruntled military chiefs waging a counterinsurgency war in the hills. Congress originally authorized funds to support the so-called Contras, but these were withdrawn under the Boland Amendments of 1985 and 1986. To keep the Contras supplied, other channels for money needed to be found by those who would have the guerilla war continue.

One of these sources was the secret traffic in arms to Iran designed to generate hard currency that became public knowledge during the Iran-Contra affair hearings. But another source of funding for the Contras may have also come from covert trading in arms and political protection to Latin American drug cartels producing cocaine. The second money channel from Colombian narcobarons might have helped oust the communists from Nicaragua, but the scam would certainly also have had a destabilizing effect on the already democratic government of Colombia.

This is not to say that the Shan did not play its part as a source of drugs-for-cash during this post-Vietnam period either, for it was by then home to the last of the Shan heirs of Chiang's military overlords, a general who went by the name of Kuhn Sa.

Kuhn Sa headed a well-equipped private army called the United Shan Army. His territory was the Golden Triangle and his business was cultivating the opium poppy and the production of heroin base for export to the West. Although Kuhn Sa's army was a formidable force, it could not have existed without the complicity of Thailand and the Laotian government, both of which (and despite the fact that Laos has a communist government) have strong ties to the United States since the Vietnam War.

Another question asked and answered by the *Factbook on Intelligence* is this: "What is the CIA's role in combating international terrorism?"

The answer is: "The Agency's counterterrorism specialists participate actively in developing strategies aimed at combating terrorism and use intelligence resources worldwide to provide significant support to U.S. efforts to solve this grave problem."

The issue of CIA sponsorship of what conspiracy theorists have dubbed "pseudoterrorism" has also been a recent charge leveled at the agency. Conspiracy theorists believe that the attacks on the World Trade Center in New York and the Alfred P. Murrah Building in downtown Oklahoma City a few years ago were acts carried out by the CIA in order to lend support to stronger counterterrorist legislation. The true purpose of such legislation, they claimed, would be to curb constitutionally protected freedoms and pave the way toward the feared national police state of the twenty-first century.[4] Nevertheless, years after the bombings, and with the zeros staring us in the face, none of these repressive measures have yet to come to pass. Gun control measures—which I as a gun enthusiast and recreational shooter personally oppose—have certainly increased, but these can be chalked up to a general trend expectable in a Democratic presidential administration.

Curiously, a president considered by conspiraholics to be a prime architect of the New World Order, George Bush, was staunchly pro-gun, even in the face of his political survival by alienating growing antigun portions of the electorate. If the New World Order wants a disarmed citizenry that it can easily enslave, then why would Bush have wanted us to keep our weapons?

Yet there is evidence that the CIA, in entering into an unholy alliance with factions of World War II's losing side, may have torn the lid off a Pandora's box of horrors and allowed the seeds of terrorism to take root at home and abroad. I'm referring here to deals the agency cut with Hitler's henchmen, the fall guys of the Third Reich's failed bid for global domination.

As the Allies closed in on Germany, the Americans and British from the West and the Soviets from the East, both sides knew there was a prize at stake whose

---

4. This does not contradict my statements in the final section of this chapter. Here I am referring to overt, systematic and widespread totalitarian repression, not the erosional process to which I later refer, and which is dangerous primarily because of its potential to culminate in police statism under the right set of circumstances.

disposition could affect the future of the world for decades to come.

This prize was the Nazi scientific brain trust that had done pioneering work in ballistic rocketry and guided missiles. Realizing that if we didn't get them first, the Soviets would, the United States spared no effort in the hunt for the Nazi rocket scientists. These were repatriated as U.S. citizens under a secret intelligence operation known as Paperclip (originally called Overcast), on the condition that they worked for the U.S. government in developing missile and rocket technology for military and civilian purposes.

Few, if any, questions were asked of these men and a blanket disavowal of a Nazi past by the recruits was usually enough to insure U.S. citizenship, good homes and high-salaried jobs in America's budding aerospace industry. Because the testing ground for Nazi rocketry was located on the German Baltic island of Peenemünde, miles from the infamous Dora-Nordhausen concentration camp complex where the missiles were actually assembled by slave labor, the fiction that the Nazi scientists were not Nazis themselves nor were aware of the hangings, beatings, shootings, starvation and torture inflicted on Dora-Nordhausen's hapless inmates was accepted.

But survivors of the camp tell a different tale. They tell of those same apolitical, non-Nazi scientists regularly witnessing atrocities committed at the camp, which was infamous for the so-called "Goat," a crane with many steel cables used for mass hangings of men guilty of infractions as trifling as stealing crusts of bread to avoid starvation. The camp's former inmates know that men such as Wernher von Braun knew all about what was happening at Dora-Nordhausen.

Not only rocket scientists, but hundreds of other former members of the SS and other rabid Nazi organizations, many of whom had participated in Nazi atrocities of all kinds, were repatriated under the CIA's Paperclip, all in the name of fighting the cold war. The CIA also cut deals with Hitler's personal enforcer Otto Skorzeny and Nazi intelligence mogul Reinhard Gehlen, who used both SS war criminals and SS booty to conduct clandestine operations for the agency (we'll get to both in a moment).

In Germany itself, the middle and lower ranks of the Nazi political and military hierarchy were left virtually intact after the leadership echelon was executed or imprisoned after the Nuremberg war crimes trials. This was also done in the name of keeping a lid on the Soviets. The Nazi managers of German industry were left in place to insure that I. G. Farben, Krupp and other industrial goliaths were put quickly back in operation after the war.

As to those Nazis, such as Mengele and Eichmann, whose presence would raise demands for immediate punishment due to the provable nature of the war crimes they had committed, special consideration was also given. Since they enjoyed the protection of those "former" Nazis deemed fit to live openly in postwar Germany, so-called "rat lines" were established with the CIA's complicity with the SS organization known as ODESSA[5], the brotherhood of ex–SS officers. Through ODESSA hundreds of other former members of Heinrich Himmler's death's head brigades found refuge in South America and the Arab world.

But the greatest blunder of all—and possibly the one with the most far-reaching consequences—involved the Eisenhower administration's co-option of a private intelligence network run by a former head of the German Abwehr to form a foreign spy network in the East Bloc of Soviet satellite states, including East Germany.

With the blessing of then–CIA director Allen Dulles, the so-called Gehlen Organization was brought into the U.S. foreign intelligence fold. Headed by Nazi spymaster Reinhard Gehlen, the network consisted mainly of ex-SS men, most of whom could have been rightfully tried for war crimes had anybody cared to take notice.

It should have been obvious that intelligence from such a ragtag group with unabashed loyalties to nazidom in exile would have been less than worthless, but apparently nobody considered this possibility at the time. The result was that the Gehlen Organization consistently produced intelligence concerning early cold war developments that, if not deliberate disinformation, was just as dangerous to global security.

As Glenn Infield points out in his book *Secrets of*

---

5. *Organisation der Entlassenen SS-Angehörigen* (Organization for the Release of Former SS Members).

the SS, the Gehlen Organization's inaccurate estimates of the progress of the Soviet Union's nuclear weapons program may have helped cause a chain reaction of nuclear proliferation that almost blew up the world, and may yet do so. Michael R. Beschloss's book, *Mayday,* also demonstrates that members of the Soviet power elite had reasons to sabotage the early Eisenhower-Khruschev detente that suddenly exploded into the full-blown cold war.

The Gehlen Organization was also penetrated by the KGB, by way of the East German intelligence agency, Stasi. This in turn infected the CIA itself with an almost viral penetration by KGB moles. Although former CIA Director of Operations James Angleton spent most of his career unsuccessfully trying to ferret out suspected (though never proven) moles, the Aldrich Ames case that surfaced in the early 1990s demonstrated that Angleton's suspicions concerning KGB penetration of the agency could have been founded on more than mere Angletonian paranoia.

The CIA deal with the survivors of the Nazi SS, and thereby with ODESSA, also indirectly supported one of the main businesses in which the Brotherhood of SS involved itself during the postwar years—training and equipping terrorist armies throughout the world, especially those supported by Libya, Syria, Iran, Iraq and Lebanon. Until his death in 1989, the head of ODESSA was one of the prime architects of covert paramilitary procedures and terrorist warfare tactics, the scar-faced Austrian enforcer named Otto Skorzeny.

Skorzeny, who was responsible for outfitting SS men

in American uniforms and inserting them behind Allied lines during the Battle of the Bulge, was one of the last Nazis to stand trial before a military court, and one of the few of the major players to be acquitted of all war crimes charges. Skorzeny, who, like Gehlen, was not unwilling to talk to reporters, boasted from his postwar residence in Barcelona, Spain, that his ODESSA forces were in league with the CIA and its affiliates in Europe, such as the then–West German BND and the French SDECE.[6]

Of course, the CIA has also directly imparted skills useful to terrorists to foreign anticommunist armies that may later have been used against the United States.

The aid given to the Afghanistani mujahideen during their 1980s war against the Soviets included training by CIA experts in special weapons, sabotage and other related covert techniques. These same ex-mujahideen— again, the fallout of a failed political movement in their homelands—may have put their lethal skills to use in the World Trade Center bombing and more recently in the anti–U.S. embassy bombings in Africa.[7]

Another question in the *Factbook* is, "Does the CIA spy on Americans? Does it keep a file on me?" The answer is, "No. The CIA is expressly prohibited by

---

6. Pronounced Seh-deek.
7. Written before September 11, 2001. Things have obviously become a lot clearer since.

presidential executive order from routinely engaging in the domestic use of such techniques as electronic, mail, or physical surveillance; monitoring devices; or uncontested physical search."

The facts argue that the CIA has at times almost certainly exceeded its mandate in domestic intelligence operations since its creation. These operations have included Cointelpro, which involved direct surveillance in the United States during the 1960s, and Mockingbird, which was established to penetrate U.S. print and electronic media with those who would disseminate pro-CIA information in news reports and opinion pieces during the 1950s and 1960s.

But the issue of domestic intelligence is largely a semantic and legalistic one, worthy of a cleric's scriptural hairsplitting. While the CIA does not have the legal right to surveil or arrest U.S. citizens in the United States, the FBI and numerous other federal, state and local police agencies certainly do possess ample, and far-reaching powers in this area, and these organizations share more than casual affiliations with one another. Further, under a program known as Echelon, the intelligence agencies of the U.S., Britain, Canada, Australia and New Zealand routinely circumvent prohibitions on domestic *electronic* spying by mutual arrangements with other governments in the program.

It is a legal fact of life that American Fifth Amendment rights against illegal search and seizure have now become eroded to the point where it is a relatively simple matter for law enforcement agencies to obtain a rubber-stamped search warrant or a court-ordered phone tap on virtually anyone.

Given the exceptionally broad wording of the Central Intelligence Agency Act of 1949, it is even arguable that by acting in a liaison capacity with local law enforcement agencies—as it very often does—the CIA could enjoy de facto domestic surveillance and arrest rights. Although these actions would overtly be taken by bona fide police agencies, the spooks would actually pull the strings in specific cases.

IMPACT ANALYSIS

Abuses by national intelligence services can result in destabilization on a global scale. This is worrisome in itself. More worrisome still is the trickle-down effect where any number of domestic intelligence units spy and eavesdrop on Americans with only borderline legal justification, contributing to an erosion of freedoms guaranteed under the U.S. Constitution and Bill of Rights. Legitimate targets of surveillance should be monitored, but the criteria for court-ordered surveillance should be tightened up to protect the rights of the majority.

VIII

Black Arsenals

Our government's array of high-technology weaponry is considered to be the most advanced in the world. Not only have Pentagon war planners made no secret of this fact, they have done everything in their power to publicize the often astonishing performance of America's weapons arsenal.

During the Gulf War, when breaking news coverage of actual fighting was nonexistent, Patriot, Stealth and other advanced weapons systems took center stage.

Today, the Web pages of U.S. Department of Defense (DOD) agencies and of the three military service branches are replete with excellent graphics, action photographs, white papers, articles and descriptions of every one of our nation's many superb weapon systems, including the secrecy-shrouded Stealth B-2 "Spirit" Bomber.

But there's nothing you'll find concerning America's nuclear arsenal. Search the Web though you may, you will find not a byte—excluding some of the missiles or ordnance that carry nuclear war loads themselves—concerning the true nuclear capability of the United States. It is missing. It is not talked about openly. It is perhaps the blackest of all black weapons programs.

And yet the nuclear arming of America has been one of the costliest and most far-reaching military programs in the history of our nation, perhaps in the history of warfare itself. To find out about it you need to consult documents prepared by such agencies as the Pentagon and the Atomic Energy Commission, many only available through the Freedom of Information Act.

An account of U.S. nuclear weapons development since World War II would easily take up a book in itself, so I'll focus on what is probably the least known aspect of the program: miniature nukes.

For decades nuclear weapons research and development has pursued a goal of cramming more and more destructive power into less and less physical space. As might be guessed from the trend in miniaturization obvious to anyone who's used a PC or cell phone, nukes have also been shrunk down to byte-sized dimensions.

Indeed research on micronukes has been at the top of the agenda at America's nuclear research laboratories, such as Los Alamos and Lawrence Livermore National Laboratories, which have been developing micronuke programs for the air force, navy and strategic command, among others. This research has paradoxically enough been driven by the end of the cold war and the downgrading and scrapping of strategic nuclear weapons per the START treaty of 1991 and others that followed.

With public and government attention diverted from the once great fear of superpower nuclear holocaust to other concerns, nuclear weapons developers have quietly, and with little oversight, been designing and building an entirely new generation of tinier and more powerful "fourth generation" nuclear weapons.

Development has proceeded under Project PLYWD (pronounced "Plywood"), which is an acronym for Precision Low-Yield Weapons Design. At the same time, combat units of all types, including infantry and special forces, have been trained in the use of these micronukes in a variety of warfare scenarios in pursuit of the project's stated goal to offer "a credible option to counter the employment of nuclear weapons by Third World nations."

Also paradoxical is the justification for the buildup of stockpiles of the new breed of micronukes—their relative nonlethality. War planners claim that because micronukes are so small, the collateral damage they would cause would be the equivalent of conventional explosives.

One military application of PLYWD nukes would be in the destruction of dams, bridges, runways, railway tunnels and other important enemy infrastructure. PLYWD nuclear weapons could also be useful, according to government proponents, in destroying enemy bunker complexes if introduced through ventilation ducts or in generating an electromagnetic pulse (EMP) and nuclear radiation to cripple enemy radars and electronic communications. In all the above cases special forces would principally be used to deliver the nuclear explosives.

All well and good, but what about the dangers to America's stated policy of nuclear nonproliferation posed by increasing stockpiles of small, concealable nuclear weapons, especially since the former Soviet Union (FSU), spurred on by U.S. PLYWD research, has been developing similar weapons of its own?

It doesn't take a degree in nuclear physics or a seat on the Joint Chiefs of Staff to surmise that micronukes would make the ideal weapons of mass destruction for terrorists. Is there a reason to believe that PLYWD nuclear munitions might find their way into the hands of terrorists or, for that matter, other types of hostile nonstate actors including organized crime cartels?

You decide: since the end of the cold war, there has been a continuing series of arrests related to the theft of weapons-grade nuclear materials in the FSU.

In 1994, Russian investigators, tailing a suspect carrying a briefcase emitting gamma radiation, arrested three men in the act of selling a container of radioactive material to a buyer on a street in the city of Kaliningrad. It was the second such incident that had occurred in a four-month period, and one case among many. More recently, Russian police seized sixty kilograms of highly enriched uranium 600 miles east of

Moscow, in the city of Izhevsk. This is enough fissionable material to make more than three Hiroshima-flavored bombs.

In the chaos of the new Russia, security at nuclear bases is a "sometimes" thing at best. Usually it's a complete sham, considering the bribe money the Russian Mafiya can afford to pay. Russian nuclear bases are guarded by so-called special installation guards, the *Okhrana Osobykh Ob'ektov* or "Triple-Os," administered by the Directorate for the Protection of Important State Objectives and Special Cargoes (OUVGOSG).

Despite the high-sounding title, it's widely known that the Triple-O is made up largely of washouts from combat units of the Russian military with few professional soldiers filling the ranks. In short, placing Triple-O guards at nuclear installations is as good as putting a sign on the door reading "Steal These Nukes—Please!"

Not that clandestine traffic is the only way that nuclear and other weapons from Russia's arsenals can make their way into the illicit arms channels of the world's weapons traffic. Russia is possibly the prime supplier of black market defense material of all kinds, and corruption is so widespread and institutionalized even under the reformist Putin administration that analysts claim that the black market and the bureaucracy are virtually one and the same.

In 1997, the Russian export agency, Rosvoorouzhenie, was accused of arms transfers of approximately $90 million without proper export licenses. As one Russian journalist put it, "It is impossible to imagine the present scale of weapon thefts from the army" in today's FSU.

On the other side of the ruble, Western nations, including the United States, are not exempt from black market arms dealing at all levels. A post–Gulf War investigation by the United Nations showed that at least thirty-five arms manufacturers, including U.S. firms, supplied a major portion of Iraq's Scud program.

There have also been several little-publicized cases of outright arms thefts from military bases in the United States over the years, such as the arms dealing ring that was discovered to be working out of Fort Bragg in 1992, selling everything from LAW rockets to .50-caliber machine guns to illicit purchasers.

Western firms are especially heavily involved with dual-use technology, which can contribute to the proliferation of another potential doomsday weapon in terrorist hands—chemical-biological weapons or CBW. According to one CIA estimate, about four hundred companies worldwide manufacture dual-use equipment that can be used to manufacture chem-bio weaponry that, according to the same report, cannot be reliably detected by currently available technical means nor can be recognized by the human senses.

The laxity of oversight of dual-use technology has contributed to the ongoing CBW programs of North Korea, Libya, Iraq and Iran. Furthermore, despite initiatives such as the U.S.-backed 1993 Chemical Weapon Convention (CWC), ratified by the U.S. Senate in April of 1997, and the internationally sponsored 1972 Biological Weapons Convention, biochemical weapons research, testing and stockpile-building continues by both rogue and "legitimate" states, the United States included.

In short, both the United States and the former Soviet Union continue to maintain comparatively large stockpiles of chemical-biological warfare agents. This is a reserve of germ and chemical weapons that may never be destroyed and can also theoretically be considered available to terrorist and criminal groups as black market goods.

What our government may know is that there are a few more nukes on the loose than it is willing to reveal to us, and that these virtually untraceable weapons are in the hands of groups that have threatened to use them against us. This may be another explanation for the widespread construction of deep underground bases across the United States noted by many conspiracy theorists.

A right-wing group was recently indicted in connection with suspected plans to turn New York City into an "uninhabitable" wasteland using home-cooked germ warfare agents. In February of 1998, former Aryan Nation member Larry Wayne Harris was arrested for allegedly conspiring to possess the toxic biological agent anthrax. In an affidavit filed in U.S. District Court in Las Vegas, FBI agents avowed that Harris had also spoken of "his plans to place a globe of bubonic plague" on the tracks of a subway station where it might be crushed by an arriving train, spreading the plague spores through the tunnel system. In 1995 Harris was arrested for illegally ordering bubonic plague microbes by mail. He pled guilty and received an eighteen-month suspended sentence.

A chemical attack by the Japanese terrorist cult group Aum Shinrikyo in the Tokyo subway in 1996 demonstrated that such statements can be more than just empty rhetoric. The Aum attack claimed three lives, and investigators found storage facilities for home-cooked toxic nerve agents at the apocalyptic sect's compound.

Next to nuclear or CB weapons, another form of attack that concerns strategic war planners thinking about potential terrorist strikes is called information attack. Although information attack has been defined by one military spokesman as any form of attack that "uses the microchip as aimpoint," it can have potential consequences almost as far-reaching as other, more high-profile weapons strikes.

Picture the chaos that would result if enemy computer hackers, during a second Mideast war five years from now, were to strike at the computer networks that millions of Americans depend on to carry out daily personal and business banking transactions. Add to this the consequences of the same far-reaching attack on mass communications of all types, including phones, email, fax, television and radio, all of which depend heavily upon computers in order to function. Also consider how such an attack might affect transportation, including commercial air travel, availability of medical care and the delivery of consumer goods.

The crippling effects of all-out information attack could, in short, have the equivalent effect of a terror bombing upon large urban populations, which is why military analysts have warned of the danger of an "electronic Pearl Harbor" stemming from infoattack.

🧩 Now, what about U.S. military weapons systems— where do they actually come from? Who designs them, builds them, tests them and later fields them in trial runs? The mechanism behind weapons development is little understood by the general public, and while not classified per se (though individual programs certainly are classified), is not held up to public scrutiny either. You say, "the Pentagon" builds the weapons, or the army builds tanks, or the navy builds ships and submarines while the air force builds planes. But what does this really mean in nuts and bolts terms?

The U.S. Department of Defense has oversight of all military weapons research and development (R&D) programs, overt and covert, including the deepest of so-called "black" or clandestine arms development programs (even this statement is an oversimplification of an extremely complex system, made for purposes of clarity). DOD functions largely as a bureaucratic layer at the top, interfacing with Congress and the president with the real engine that drives U.S. defense R&D, an agency called DARPA, which stands for the Defense Advanced Research Projects Agency.

Though its name evokes a perception of secrecy in many, there is nothing secret about the existence of DARPA. In fact, it has its own Web site that will tell you about many of its ongoing programs. At this writing, it is run by a very congenial guy, Director Larry Lynn, who has even been known to crack funny jokes on occasion. DARPA is a unique government agency in that it is a hybrid of military and civilian personnel. Much of DARPA's work is done at what are known as applied research laboratories, often located at prestigious universities that receive government funding to carry on weapons research.

In fact, many of these civilian laboratories are located on military bases, such as Rome Lab, a facility engaged in a great deal of secret weapons research at Griffiss Air Force base in upstate New York. While military staff officers oversee this work, it is largely carried out by civilians who have high security clearances.

There is a special culture to which these civilian researchers belong. They frequently view themselves as a breed apart, privy to secrets far beyond the understanding of the ordinary citizen. In fact, they are the real-life equivalents of the archetypal "mad scientist" of fiction who can display a distinctly Strangelovian bent, such as two overheard at a recent military symposium discussing "the next step," which would be, "grafting the camera directly onto the human eyeball . . ."

The role DARPA plays is to develop prototype weapon systems for applications defined by the armed service branches or the DOD in what is known by the current buzzword "technological push-pull." This simply means that a need creates a "push" that results in an R&D "pull" in the form of a new system.

In the case of stealth, for example, the need to reduce observability of aircraft to enemy radars was the push that resulted in the pull of the various technologies that comprise stealth. During the process of prototype development, DARPA, in conjunction with the military, carries out ACTDs, or advanced concept technology demonstrations. When the ACTD trials are completed, the weapon system is "rolled out" or turned over to the military end user.

It's believed that for most overt or "white world" DARPA programs there is an equivalent black or covert program that exploits some or all of the publicly revealed technology. In fact, it is thought that some of the open programs with which DARPA is involved are actually covers for clandestine research going on behind the scenes.

Often, a white program will be canceled or be shut down due to "lack of funding" or because "political developments no longer warrant it" only to continue in its clandestine development mode, very much alive and producing arcane technologies that will form the basis for new breeds of secret weapons. One of the reasons such programs go underground is because even acknowledging the existence of a revolutionary new technology with important military applications can give adversaries clues to how to mimic or defeat it.

Stealth technology, now openly acknowledged, though for years one of DARPA's most closely guarded secrets, is one example. A more current example of the above may be the existence of hypersonic aviation technologies based on years of DARPA research. The so-called Aurora Project is believed by many to have produced a revolutionary space plane capable of transiting the earth at the edge of space at multimach speeds.

■ One of the major weapons system initiatives ever undertaken by DARPA was the development of the many separate technologies that went into SDI, an acronym for Strategic Defense Initiative, otherwise known as Star Wars. Officially canceled at the end of the cold war, and then reactivated on a "limited basis," it is believed by some that SDI research has never actually been curtailed but has simply become shrouded in secrecy as a clandestine project.

A comprehensive account of the separate technologies that make up SDI would be beyond the scope of this book. Essentially SDI is an array of networked space- and ground-based systems that include hyperkinetic/hypervelocity weapons, particle beam weapons and laser weapons, all of which are linked to a network of computers and sensors that assess the nature and level of threat and determine by what means to respond.

The first class of weapons, hyperkinetic/hypervelocity, use electromagnetic energy to propel projectiles of various kinds at extremely high speeds. The second class, particle beam weapons, also exploit the electromagnetic spectrum to attack targets with concentrated beams of destructive energy. The third class, laser weapons, work in a similar manner, but are limited to close-in attack since they don't perform well through atmospheric cloud cover.

Conspiracy theorists believe that SDI weapons were never developed as the "defense umbrella" against nuclear attack that they were publicly described as being. Instead they claim that SDI's primary purpose was to act as a defense shield against alien spacecraft.[1]

It's also claimed that proof of the true nature of SDI lies in the relative alacrity with which the Soviets unilaterally disarmed themselves in the early 1990s, as by then much of the U.S. SDI umbrella was in position. Some proponents of this view have been highly placed.

Whether this is true or not, it's based on the mistaken assumption that the Soviets were not developing an SDI technology base of their own while we were building ours. But the Soviets were without a doubt very hard at work on their own SDI, and U.S. military intelligence knew all about these Russian Star Wars efforts from an early stage.

In fact, declassified KGB and GRU documents reveal that the Soviets were hard at work on SDI well before our own Star Wars research began. Furthermore, U.S. efforts could have been an attempt to "close the SDI gap" as a previous era had once tried to close a "missile gap."

Soviet SDI research began as early as 1969 with efforts to develop directed energy weapons including strategic and tactical laser weapons for basing in space,

---

1. The same assertion is now being made for the current National Missile Defense (NMD) initiative.

on the ground and on aircraft, ships and vehicles.

A second phase of Soviet SDI involved the development of an array of what FSU documents call "space strike systems," including a network of space stations armed with laser cannons and other directed energy weapons for orbital strikes, and missiles for use against atmospheric or ground targets.

These systems were to occupy various levels of the orbital plane between low and high orbit, right out to the critical L-7 point midway between the earth and the moon. The Soviet space battle stations would be capable of operating in either manned or unmanned modes and be able to strike targets in space or on earth. Unlike U.S. efforts, which were mostly aimed at knocking out incoming nuclear ballistic missiles, the Soviet plan was far broader in scope, with offensive and defensive capabilities alike.

Currently on the hate list of conspiracy theorists is an SDI weapon known as HAARP, which stands for High Frequency Active Auroral Research Project. Physically, HAARP is an array of antennae that are capable of beaming directed energy into the upper atmosphere. The official position of DOD is that HAARP is designed to create survivable military communications linkages between military forces despite any form of attack, including nuclear.

One of HAARP's roles is to insure more secure communications between nuclear ballistic submarine forces than that which currently exists, considered especially important due to the role nuclear subs will play as the primary leg of U.S. strategic nuclear forces in the twenty-first century. HAARP does this by injecting high frequency radio waves into the ionosphere, an electrically charged region at the outermost layer of the earth's atmosphere. These waves generate virtual "lenses" or "mirrors" capable of reflecting a variety of radio frequencies far over the horizon.

This capability would enable radars to see much farther out than they currently can and recognize new breeds of stealthy weapons that can fly at very low altitudes, such as stealth aircraft and cruise missiles. It would also greatly enhance communication with the far-flung submarines forming the sea-based leg of the U.S. nuclear triad by transmitting ELF (extra low frequency) radio signals over the horizon. HAARP could also create a global missile defense shield of high energy through which enemy missiles (some say alien spacecraft) would have to pass before reaching the earth.

That's the nutshell of what HAARP is officially. Critics call it something else and claim that HAARP is in fact a doomsday weapon with an entirely different purpose and set of capabilities. The same high frequency radio energies that HAARP uses for long-range communications purposes could cause irreparable harm to the earth's atmosphere and also be used to beam various forms of energies down to earth as so-called "psychotronic" weapons.

The same ELF waves that would be bounced off the virtual mirrors to communicate with submarines are also claimed to be useful in mind control efforts, especially when used in conjunction with various otherwise harmless chemical substances that act synergistically with the low frequency radio waves.

These substances could supposedly be prereleased into the water and food supplies from which, in conjunction with HAARP radiation, they would enable psychotronic control over target populations. Conspiracy theorists claim that this has been already happening for some time now, and explains much of the craziness pervading our society, a mass madness that has been engineered by a conspiracy intending to destroy our ability to reason and our will to resist an impending coup d'etat.

IMPACT ANALYSIS

Though some claims of secret weapons programs sound farfetched, there are others that are more believable and chilling in their own right. The virtually unregulated, decades-long development of nuclear weapons is tantamount to a cover-up of major proportions. It has created a field sown with dragon's teeth, both in the proliferation of many forms of very compact and portable nuclear weapons, and in the clear and present danger that some of these may have already fallen into the hands of terrorist or criminal organizations at home and abroad.

IX 🧩

Secret Bases

At the conclusion of Stanley Kubrick's 1964 film *Dr. Strangelove*, the character of the same name consoles the U.S. president and his key advisors as the world faces imminent nuclear holocaust. Taking out his slide rule, Dr. Strangelove calculates that the toxic radioactivity on the earth's surface will subside in about one hundred years, at which time the world can be repopulated.

In the meantime, not to worry. There are secret underground facilities for the nation's elite where the chosen few can spend their lifetimes in security and comfort, breeding a new (and maybe better) human race. In fact, says Strangelove, to speed up the breeding process, every man should be provided with ten women as sex partners. This especially appeals to the film's General Buck Turgidson, said to be a parody of the actual head of the U.S. Strategic Air Command at the time, General Curtis LeMay.

In the James Bond films, both the good guys (Her Majesty's Secret Service) and the bad guys (Spectre or Smersh) had secret underground bases. Dr. No's base was even located underwater. Fortunately for 007, most of these bases were equipped with convenient air shafts leading to the surface through which Bond could always crawl to safety (and the embraces of beautiful women).

More recently, two box office hits dealing with alien invaders, *Independence Day* and *Men in Black,* featured super-secret hidden bases. The former was a Hollywood mock-up of an Area 51–type installation, the latter was hidden underneath a building recognizable to this author as one of the giant ventilation shafts for the Holland Tunnel in New York City, though never identified as such in the film (although the tunnel itself played a starring role).

The notion of secret bases is linked to the idea of hidden worlds and underground civilizations. It dates back to the nineteenth century, when Edgar Rice Burroughs and Jules Verne first popularized it in books such as *The Lost Continent, Journey to the Center of the Earth* and *From the Earth to the Moon.*

But it was World War II that saw the first genuine examples of secret underground facilities that later became public knowledge. These bases were made necessary on both sides of the conflict by the emergence of air power, coupled with highly accurate bombsighting, as a major factor in the war. Critical war installations had to be made bombproof in order to survive, and the only way to effectively do this was to move them underground—the deeper underground the better.

On the Allied side, the British set up several underground installations. One, the Cabinet war rooms directly below the streets of central London, has been preserved as a war museum and is today open to the public. A far more extensive underground facility on the German side, the rocketry works at Nordhausen, in the Harz Mountains of northeastern Germany, has also been recently opened as a war museum.

The Nordhausen complex was a vast underground network of immense concrete tunnels and huge factory bunkers. These served the construction of V-1 cruise missiles and V-2 ballistic missiles (the mother of all Scuds, which are latter-day offspring of the V-2) that not even the heaviest Allied blockbuster bombs could seriously damage.

In the postwar years, the United States and the Soviet Union both began the process of building underground installations intended to withstand the tremendously destructive blast effects of high-yield nuclear weapons. In the United States the headquarters of the Strategic Air Command (now STRATCOM) was built beneath Offutt Air Force Base at Omaha, Nebraska (some say directly beneath a famous oak tree) and the U.S.-Canadian NORAD (North American Aerospace Defense Command) complex was established inside the hollowed-out granite core of Cheyenne Mountain, Colorado.

The NORAD complex is an incredible piece of engineering work. The facility is made up of fifteen steel office buildings mounted atop a series of gargantuan springs and shock absorbers anchored onto the roots of the mountain. Seven thousand tons of steel were needed to construct the buildings and nearly 700,000 tons of granite had to be excavated to make room for them.

A 4,675-foot, north-south tunnel bored end to end through the mountain links the complex's main bunker with the outside world. The tunnel was designed as a kind of pressure release valve for the heat and blast overpressure produced by a nuclear strike, and also to afford a back door if one exit were buried under blast rubble. These features and two twenty-five-ton hydraulically operated blast doors made of three-foot-thick steel plates on the mountain's western face are among the many features intended to help NORAD survive even a direct hit by a multi-megaton nuclear warhead.

Other known underground installations in the United States include the Pacific Fleet Operations Control Center at Kunia, Hawaii, the Alternate National Military Command Center at Raven Rock, Maryland, and the Manzano Mountain nuclear weapons storage base at Albuquerque, New Mexico, among others. Similar known underground facilities in foreign countries include the NATO Command Center at Boerfink, Germany, the Alternate National Military Command Center at Mt. Verdun, France, the NCA Command Post at Hohhot, China, and the Situation Room and Military Command Post located directly beneath the Kremlin.

A far more clandestine counterpart of these bases is said to be the above-mentioned Area 51, a part of the Groom Lake installation in Nevada run by the USAF. One well-publicized account by an eyewitness claims that alien spacecraft and alien technologies are in evidence at Area 51. Whether true or not, the surrounding countryside has for years become a gathering place for groups of sightseers, conspiracy theorists and UFO buffs, and reports of strange occurrences at night are common.

■ But what about the truth of secret bases? Do they exist and, if so, what is going on inside them? And in the event that they truly do exist, then why haven't we been told of their existence? Let's examine some of the claims.

First and foremost, there is Area 51, a facility seen in satellite photos as a three-mile-long runway, expanses of low, hangar-style buildings and clusters of radar dishes and antennae resting on the dry bed of a fossil lake—Groom Lake, to be exact—which gives the facility one of its several names.

Area 51, otherwise known as Dreamland and The Ranch, is located in the northeast section of the U.S. government's sprawling Nevada Test Site at Mercury, Nevada. The site, bordered by the imposing mass of the nearby Groom Mountains, is located approximately sixty-five miles north of Nellis Air Force Base and has figured in the development of several special aircraft that were kept secret for a long time. These include the B-2 Stealth bomber and the still-mysterious SR-71 "Blackbird" reconnaissance aircraft program, one that remains classified more than thirty years after the existence of the SR was made public.

Although Area 51 is not all that far from the bright Las Vegas lights in pure highway miles, to all intents and purposes it might as well be located on the far side of the moon. The surrounding desert terrain is sparsely populated and ill-traveled. Those who live in the vicinity tend to keep their mouths shut and their minds on their own business. It goes with the territory, as they say.

But droves of outsiders have a different attitude. They hold vigils from observation points on the Groom Mountains that overlook parts of Area 51 where they claim evidence of flight tests of alien spacecraft can frequently be seen as strange lights moving across the pitch-black night skies. At this writing, for instance, gatherings are being organized by local conspiracy watch groups to observe the goings-on at the installation on the dry lake below—it happens all the time.

There has been a tantalizing insider's glimpse of Area 51 too. In 1989, a man named Robert Lazar went public with what seemed at the time to be incredible revelations concerning a super-secret government program involving alien technologies based at Area 51. Lazar's story is still controversial and has yet to be definitively proven or successfully debunked.

At the time Lazar was a civilian physicist under contract with the U.S. Navy. He was employed in research work at what he claims was a super-secret facility called S-4, a few miles south of Groom Lake. S-4 was allegedly built into the side of a mountain and had a giant hangar door camouflaged to look like the surrounding desert sand. He and co-workers were first flown to Groom Lake and then driven to S-4 in a bus with blacked-out windows, Lazar claims.

Inside S-4, Lazar said there were flying saucers, antimatter reactors and other forms of bizarre alien technology. He stated that there were nine saucers in all at the clandestine facility, each one of them different, and most of them looking brand-new, as if, in his words, they had been acquired as part of an exchange program. He also stated that slick posters decorated the walls showing a flying saucer and the caption, "They're here."

At one point Lazar got a demonstration of a disk-shaped saucer he identified as the "Sport Model,"[1] which he saw lift off the hangar floor, fly noiselessly around the hangar and then settle back down. At another point, he claimed to have briefly glimpsed an alien or extraterrestrial biological entity (EBE).

Lazar claimed to have gone public when he discov-

---

1. Lazar claims the Sport Model is identical to one of the saucers depicted in a series of photographs taken by Swiss UFO contactee Eduard Meir. These color photographs are not only the clearest ever publicly available of UFOs but they have also never been convincingly proven to have been faked.

ered that the physical evidence of his past life was being systematically erased by unknown actors and he feared that this might be a prelude to his own eventual bodily disappearance.

Regular intimidation by an enforcement staff at S-4, including threats at gunpoint, convinced him that he was dealing with individuals who stopped at nothing. Lazar also claimed concern about the way the program was being conducted—after some forty years of secret investigations into alien technology, government researchers had accomplished little and it was time to throw the doors open to unrestricted research, according to Lazar.

An even stranger and still more disturbing story concerning a secret base involves what is known as "the underground city" said to be located in the vicinity of Dulce, New Mexico. This subterranean installation is said to be a sprawling multilevel facility tunneled out of the earth beneath the desert floor by giant burrowing machines using a nuclear heating system to bore tunnels with smooth, glazed walls.

Such a process doesn't leave tons of rock and dirt behind, say conspiracy theorists. The facility is purported to extend far underground to an extensive depth. The facility is also said to be connected to the Los Alamos nuclear weapons plant by an underground tube shuttle.

The Dulce base is supposedly home to a mixed population of aliens (18,000 from one report!) from a variety of planetary systems, including Greys from Orion and Zeta Reticuli, and terran humans. It was said to have originated as a consequence of a human-alien pact in the wake of the Roswell saucer crash (see following chapters). Signs of construction were first noticed by locals in the summer of 1947, around the time of the Roswell incident, especially heavy trucks bearing the words "Smith Corporation," a nonexistent firm in 1947.

The Dulce tunnel complex supposedly has all the comforts anyone could want—from this planet or any other. It's completely outfitted with apartment blocks and shopping malls with stores catering to humans and aliens alike. But that doesn't mean it's a subterranean Beverly Hills. The complex reportedly extends downward for seven levels, possibly more than seven, with aliens occupying the lowest three. The facility is dedicated to the development of biogenetic programming projects by both aliens and humans.

One of the fruits of these projects is said to be the creation by humans of synthetic biological entities— bioengineered androids resembling the drone entities allegedly used by alien races to pilot spacecraft, perform human abductions, and other remote operations deemed too dangerous or risky to carry out directly.

Like the aliens themselves, human-engineered synthetics are created from fetuses purloined from the wombs of pregnant women and subjected to advanced forms of DNA manipulation and programming. The drone entities are wired up with alien-developed implant technology inserted into the head via the nose, and controlled by means of RHIC, or radio-hypnotic intracerebral memory technology. It is believed that the so-called "men in black" (see following chapter) are actually these synthetic entities.

In the deepest levels of the Dulce complex is located what has become known to conspiraholics as "Nightmare Hall." These are the sections housing laboratory facilities where research into advanced genetics is carried out.

In level 6, human-animal and other hybrid beings are reportedly kept in cages. Below, in level 7, there are said to be thousands of humans, human hybrids, and embryonic forms, kept in cold storage. Cattle mutilations, common in the surrounding area adjacent to the base, are said to provide living cell tissue and blood used for genetic research and manipulation. The blood is also used as food by certain alien races, it is claimed.

Security at the Dulce base—as at other similar bases said to be scattered below the surface of the U.S. Southwest—is said to be maintained by elements of Delta Force. In fact, it is alleged that Delta Force— ostensibly created for counterterrorist operations—was in fact formed expressly as a terran strike force to engage in counter-alien operations; in this view counterterrorism is only a sideline for Delta.[2]

Delta Force personnel assigned to alien operations

---

2. It's real hard for me to believe that Colonel Charles Beckwith, who succeeded in creating Delta Force, against great bureaucratic resistance, and over a period of many years, would have been part of an alien cover-up scam, willingly, unwillingly, or otherwise. To me this particular assertion sounds like a joke.

such as security at the Dulce base are believed to wear badges and patches showing a black triangle on a red background (ID cards given to Dulce personnel are said to bear the Great Seal of the Republic). Delta Force personnel are also supposedly among those flying the much-feared black helicopters of conspiracy lore.

Can secret bases like those cited above really exist? Or are they complete figments of the imagination? In this regard it might be useful to take a look at a secret base about whose existence there is hard evidence, and which, though it has nothing to do with aliens, is astonishing in its own right.

Mount Weather, located some forty-eight miles from the nation's capital, outside Berryville, Virginia, is a secret and secure underground shelter built to protect the elite of the United States government from catastrophic environmental disaster and acts of war, up to and including nuclear attack. It is operated by FEMA, the Federal Emergency Management Agency.

There is no way to consider Mount Weather a figment of anyone's imagination. Like the buried bunker systems of NORAD and STRATCOM, it definitely exists, though its existence is not officially acknowledged. FEMA's published budget makes no mention of Mount Weather, the facility has no street address, and the agency's official response to inquiries about the facility is a blunt "no comment."

Originally used as a government weather station at

the turn of the century, the site was adopted during World War II as a testbed for deep-drilling technology by the U.S. Bureau of Mines. The original tunnel, some three hundred feet long, seven feet high and six and a half feet wide, became the nucleus of the present day tunnel complex, probably begun after the 1949 detonation of the first Soviet atomic bomb.

By 1954, work by the Bureau of Mines was underway to expand the original tunnel into a vast network of bunkers and side tunnels that would ultimately house electric power stations, secure command centers, living quarters for staff, a hospital, a cafeteria, a TV recording studio, and many other related facilities.

In addition to these, underground lakes were excavated from the living rock, some estimated at ten feet deep and two hundred feet across. Some were used as reservoirs for drinking water, others as part of a cooling system for the system's array of high-speed mainframe computers.

An air shaft running down from the mountaintop was also excavated and equipped with massive blowers and pumps to provide breathable air to the complex, and a five-foot-thick blast door measuring twenty feet across protected by a rapid-closing guillotine gate was installed to quickly and securely seal off the facility from any anticipated external threat.

Since the facility was built, there has been a permanent support staff assigned to Mount Weather, which continues to serve its original purpose despite the end of the cold war and the fading away of the threat that it was originally built to withstand. The on-site staff of about 250 includes the headquarters of the National Emergency Coordination Center, an agency that monitors disasters around the world whether natural or man-made.

And also today, as at the start of the cold war, handpicked officials of the U.S. government stand ready to rehearse an evacuation drill that will prepare them for the real thing, should it ever happen.

Most of these privileged "evacuees" carry special identification cards that command preferential treatment by police, military and other emergency personnel in the event of national emergency, and the evacuees are regularly briefed on emergency assemblage points for rapid rescue operations that would spirit them to Mount Weather in times of trouble.

In one published example of this procedure, William Brock, the Reagan administration's labor secretary from 1985 to 1987, was an evacuee high on the priority list due to his ranking of eleventh on the roll of presidential successors. Brock, who stated that he never went anywhere without his evacuee card, was whisked by helicopter one day from the center of Washington, D.C., and flown directly to Mount Weather, to the astonishment of onlookers.

This sounds comforting for the few hundred privileged members of government holding evacuee cards, but what about the rest of the nation's approximately two hundred eighty million citizens? Where would they go and what would they do in the event of a catastrophic emergency, such as a nuclear attack?

Let's look at a telling statistic: in the years since

construction of the Mount Weather facility began, the U.S. government has spent an estimated $60 million alone on maintenance and upgrading of the facility and millions more on evacuation plans and procedures in the event of emergency.

Compare this with the virtual absence of infrastructure to prepare and protect the average U.S. citizen against war, terrorism and natural disaster—the United States government spends only about thirty-five cents a head per year on civil defense.

While the chosen few can expect to be winged to safety, the ordinary taxpayer is told, as in a recent FEMA brochure called *Are You Prepared?*, to build fallout shelters from "common household items" and take his or her chances on surviving nuclear or other cataclysmic attack.

It can also be inferred that emergency evacuation personnel, such as Secret Service agents and military special operations personnel, would have orders to exclude anyone but the evacuees by whatever means available—remember the video footage of the fall of Saigon in 1975 if you entertain doubts about what those "means" might conceivably turn out to entail.

To spell it out for you, this strongly suggests that if your wife and kids happened to be in the vicinity of a Bush administration staff member with an evacuee card, they could well be pushed aside, and if they demanded a ride on the magic helicopter to safety, they might well be beaten back or shot down in cold blood. Orders are orders, especially in a severe emergency—presumably even orders to kill.

Add to this grim scenario what any expert on nuclear warfare will tell you: *there is no sure way to protect a facility like Mount Weather from obliteration by all-out nuclear attack, given the accuracy and power of today's thermonuclear weapons.* There is also no reason to assume that such a large-scale attack would leave a governable population in its wake and very many reasons to believe that society as we know it would be all but wiped out in the process. The same could be said concerning an attack using many types of biological or chemical weapons.

What this boils down to is that the super-bunker for America's elite is incapable of fulfilling the mission for which it was designed—unless the real nature of that mission happens to be the same one proposed by Dr. Strangelove in a movie subtitled *How I Stopped Worrying and Learned to Love the Bomb.*

IMPACT ANALYSIS

The existence of secret bases within the United States is one of the cornerstones of conspiracy theory. Whether or not any of the taller tales of these secret bases are true, the fact remains that at least one such underground base, the Mount Weather complex, actually does exist. What's more, the base exists to serve the survival interests of a chosen few. While leadership must be maintained in time of national crisis, if America is indeed "one nation, under God," then Mount Weather is if nothing else symbolic of the opposite of one of our most cherished national ideals.

X

The Roswell Cover-up

Ranking on the disbelief scale next to the official explanations offered for the JFK-RFK-MLK shootings is the leeriness of government denunciations concerning UFO phenomena and alien encounters. It has reached the point where official pronouncements are scoffed at by a majority of people, and that the existence of government-alien pacts and alliances stretching back to at least 1947, though heatedly denied, is nevertheless considered an open secret by many.

Various polls reveal that most Americans believe UFOs and aliens are real and that the U.S. government is deliberately hiding the truth from them. This is astonishing considering that public opinion has done a complete one-eighty from the unconditional acceptance of the immediate postwar years to the near-total skepticism of today. But maybe it's not so astonishing when you consider the mass of disinformation that has been offered the public concerning everything from MIAs to the safety of the foods we eat. Ultimately unconditional acceptance turns into something close to its opposite: reflex suspicion.

One of the stories that refuses to go away concerns the crash of an extraterrestrial spacecraft in the vicinity of Roswell, New Mexico, on or about July 4, 1947.

It's believed by many UFOlogists that the Roswell event is connected with the alleged earlier sighting of another downed discoid spacecraft approximately 150 miles to the west, in a region of the high desert near the city of Albuquerque called the Plains of San Augustin.

It's thought that the two spacecraft may have collided with one another during one of the fierce electrical storms that often sweep across the desert during the summer months and that the crews of both vehicles lost control.[1] Whatever the cause of the events, it's

---

1. One of the first things debunkers, such as the late Carl Sagan, use against stories of alleged saucer crashes, is that spacecraft built by supercivilizations wouldn't crash so easily. This is not an airtight rebuttal. A billion-dollar Stealth bomber, a plane representing the highest aviation technology on the planet, is not less but *more* susceptible to damage from relatively minor hazards. Problems that would not phase the B-52 bomber, a dinosaur by comparison, could down the B-2 very quickly. It's not that much of a conceptual leap to posit the same for advanced spacecraft.

certain that objects came down out of the skies leaving behind burning contrails. The objects were believed to have been meteors by the many observers on the ground who reported sightings of the phenomena.

It's also certain that the USAF was extremely interested in getting its hands on those objects and rushing them—and any crash debris—away from the crash site as hastily as possible, and that intelligence personnel were equally determined to bully and threaten any crash witnesses into silence in the weeks and months following the events.

In September of 1994, the USAF released the latest of several updated reports on the Roswell incident. The report stated that the debris found in New Mexico in 1947 probably came from the then–highly classified Project Mogul, a high-altitude balloon carrying cameras and sensors used to monitor evidence of Soviet nuclear tests in the days before surveillance satellites performed this function. The explanation is, to many observers, less than convincing.

For one thing, the level of brute force used by the military to disperse civilians who had arrived on scene before the search and recovery teams, and to cordon off the area, seems excessive even for a top-secret project like Mogul. Reports by eyewitnesses all agree that military personnel arrived carrying loaded weapons and were ready to use them on the locals. Of course there are also accounts from apparently reliable eyewitnesses concerning the nature of the crash as well.

At the San Augustin site observers reported a saucer-shaped spacecraft approximately fifty feet in diameter and silver in color, which had crashed diagonally into the side of a hill and the presence of four alien beings of short stature, all but one either injured or dead.

At the site of the Roswell crash, the spacecraft was described as smaller and with a black hull. It was not described as a typical saucer but as a distorted crescent with two outward-pointing fins at left and right of the fuselage rear. Here too, alien beings in various states of injury were supposedly found by those who first arrived on scene.

In addition to the saucer in the Roswell incident, the crash site was reportedly strewn with a field of debris that had broken loose from the spacecraft as it made a low-trajectory descent into the side of yet another New Mexican hill.

Persons who arrived at the scene ahead of the military reported picking up strange and unearthly objects from this debris field. Once the military arrived, search teams were dispatched to comb the desert for every last scrap of alien detritus. Civilian bystanders were ordered to turn over anything they'd found. Most did, but those who kept their finds said they were later bullied into giving up these artifacts as well.

Those of us who've followed modern media coverage of jetliner crashes—such as the Lockerbie crash of 1987, where a TWA commercial flight was blown up by a terrorist bomb, strewing the Scottish highlands with a similar debris field to that described at Roswell—are familiar with the painstaking difficulty of recovering all fragments of crash debris. Such work can normally take up to several days. Yet here a frantic search was immediately begun.

It seems unlikely that the military would make the kind of effort it did for a mere observation balloon, no matter how classified its mission. The most persuasive explanation for the military's actions would be that the crash was too sensitive a matter for even a hint of its existence to reach the Soviets, so extraordinary care needed to be taken to protect the secret.

The only problem with this assessment is that the Soviets knew all about the efforts that the United States was making to monitor their fledgling nuclear weapons program, just as they knew all about the U-2 and SR-71 spy plane projects that succeeded early nuclear intelligence gathering initiatives such as Mogul.

The KGB, via the so-called Gehlen Organization, the already mentioned prepackaged spy network run by ex–Nazi Abwehr agent Reinhard Gehlen, had penetrated U.S. intelligence infrastructure by this time, and the Soviets were very well informed about most of America's supposedly best-kept intelligence secrets. Of special concern to Russia would be those efforts directed at surveilling their military weapons development programs. Therefore, it's highly unlikely that the observation balloon explanation is the real one for the actions of the military in the New Mexico desert near the end of the Truman presidency.

Then what is? In a recent book called *The Day After Roswell*, retired army Colonel Philip J. Corso makes a forceful case for an alternative explanation. Corso asserts that what crashed at Roswell was in fact an alien spacecraft from which four alien bodies were retrieved—the lone survivor having been "shot while trying to escape," to quote a line from an old Bogie film.

According to Corso, radar operators attached to the USAF's 209th fighter wing had been monitoring the Roswell UFO on their scopes during a fierce electrical storm prior to the crash, and when the weird blip (weird because of the way it behaved) disappeared off the screens, a search and retrieval team was immediately dispatched to the assumed crash site. What the team found there was exactly what had been expected—a downed alien craft, much like the one previously located at San Augustin and, some claim, like those found at other crash sites prior to the New Mexican crashes.

Even as the teams went to work, a massive counter-intelligence operation was launched to cover up the reality of what had happened—the fact that alien technology of radically advanced design was now in the hands of the United States. As Corso tells it, it was this and nothing else that the United States was so intent on keeping from the Soviets.

At this stage of the game the Soviets had achieved a rough parity with U.S. efforts to develop high-technology weapons systems, especially advanced ballistic missile systems capable of intercontinental ranges. Both the United States and Soviet Russia had built their rocket and jet technology base from the spoils of Nazi research and development.

By the end of the war, scientists of the Third Reich had developed the Messerschmitt Me 262A series jet fighter, a stealthy flying wing (the so-called Horton wing), a rocket plane, and sea-launch versions of the V-1 and V-2 missiles capable of being launched from new long-range U-boats.[2] Hitler's threatened use of Nazi superweapons to snatch victory from the jaws of defeat, if an idle boast, was nevertheless based on fact. If fully functional superweapons were not available, the technology base from which they could have been built, had Germany been given more time, was actually there.

As the Allies closed in on Berlin in the spring of 1945, a feverish hunt was underway to locate this advanced Nazi technology and the scientists that had been working on it. American forces won the race by reaching the German rocketry proving grounds on the German Baltic island of Peenemünde and the underground assembly plant at nearby Nordhausen.

Under the covert project called Operation Paperclip, former Nazi scientists were quietly repatriated as U.S. citizens irrespective of their war crimes and put to work developing America's space and missile technology programs. But the Soviet Union got the remainder of the technology and talent, enough to bring their own programs abreast of the West's.

---

2. The "rocket planes" came in several models. One was a souped-up V-1 "buzz bomb" with a cramped pilot's cockpit. The "planes" were extremely difficult to steer, which is why pilots had to sign a release stating that they took the job with the full knowledge that it would result in their deaths. Only test firings of the sea-launched V-2 took place.

According to Corso, with the retrieval of Roswell technology all this changed in an instant. The United States now had the beginnings of an entirely new set of innovations. Even if the Americans couldn't completely grasp it yet, the Soviets would have surmised that in time U.S. researchers could piece the puzzle together.

The need to hide the full extent of what was recovered from the Roswell crash site from the Soviets was one of the reasons for the UFO coverup that supposedly followed—a cover-up mandated by then-President Truman in whose service an entirely new security clearance was created. Another was the fear of mass hysteria on the part of government planners in the wake of the Orson Welles's radio broadcast of H. G. Wells's *War of the Worlds,* which had earlier caused widespread panic.

The third reason for the alleged cover-up was the dawning awareness by government officials that extraterrestrial biological entities (EBEs) possessing awesome technology were buzzing our most highly classified military installations with impunity, kidnapping human beings for unknown purposes and killing and mutilating our livestock, and there wasn't anything we could do about it. These EBEs were not from any one particular planet, but comprised a variety of races from several star systems, it was believed.

Some UFO researchers claim that as time went on the U.S. government entered into an ultrasecret pact with at least some alien races under a program known as Majic. The arrangement provided U.S. research and development initiatives with alien technology—including flying disks—in return for a free hand in kidnapping and experimenting on humans. As the involvement deepened, it was imperative to keep the cover-up in place. By then too many careers and reputations had been put on the line.

Corso does contend that the alien technology recovered from the Roswell crash formed the basis for an array of weapons systems that have enabled humans to fight back against the invading aliens and prevent them from taking over the planet, as was their intention.

According to the colonel, the true reason behind Strategic Defense Initiative or Star Wars was not to create an antiballistic missile defense shield but to orbit a weapons array capable of targeting and destroying alien spacecraft before they reached the earth. This, coupled with a satellite surveillance program to detect hidden alien bases even in remote corners of the planet, is the reason why humans continue to dominate our world today.

Finally, Corso contends that technologies recovered from the Roswell crash formed the basis not only for today's "smart" weapons systems but for consumer goods that are currently commonplace but were virtually undreamed of back in 1947. Among these is the integrated circuit chip, the component that makes possible everything from laptops to talking anniversary cards. Another is the laser. A third is infrared night vision technology.

All of these were said to have been recovered from the Roswell crash and afterward secretly given to major defense contractors who reverse-engineered them to determine how they worked and how they could be plugged into existing R&D programs. Corso seems gratified about how it all worked out in the end, but if his claims are credible, they raise questions of propriety on the part of U.S. industry and government policy.

If these alien technologies—technologies which literally "fell from the sky"—were given to commercial firms on a royalty-free basis, and these same firms were permitted to patent technologies that stemmed from these found alien artifacts that had fallen on public lands in the middle of the New Mexican desert, then wouldn't they rightfully become public property instead of the "intellectual property" that large corporations have guarded so jealously?

Also, before taking the colonel at his word, we need to know more about his background, especially concerning his past record of associations with organizations and individuals, and about other statements he might have made in the past concerning conspiracies of various kinds.

IMPACT ANALYSIS

The Roswell crash continues to excite the public's imagination and confound efforts to positively debunk it. If a cover-up exists, its exposure could have truly cosmic implications for the human race. But is humanity prepared for revelations of such magnitude? If Watergate, Irangate and even Monicagate have sent shock waves rippling through our culture, what would the impact of a full accounting of Roswell be like? In some ways it might be better if the lid was kept on Roswell for some time to come—but at least let the air force come up with something better than a "crashed weather balloon."

XI 🧩

Alien Nation

As already mentioned in connection with Roswell, one of the most persistent of all conspiracy theories concerns the alleged decades-long government cover-up of the truth about aliens among us. Government-sponsored studies, such as the USAF's Project Bluebook and the Condon Report, have repeatedly insisted there's no such thing as aliens, at least not the kind that abduct humans for genetic experimentation, mind control and other nefarious purposes.

There may be aliens light-years away, in distant reaches of the galaxy, but humans will have to find them in order to establish contact. Apparently, according to the official line, it can't work the other way around. Somehow, the notion that aliens would covertly come to our planet, without announcing their presence in some grandiose manner, isn't a workable concept for the political and scientific establishment.

That extraterrestrials would choose to infiltrate themselves into human society or remain behind the scenes in order to serve ends unknown to the earth's inhabitants, or that they would have the technological resources to do this for as long as they wanted, is not worth considering. This is something like the humpback whales saying that Jacques Cousteau never existed and that the Calypso can be explained by "weather balloons or other natural phenomena."

The only two reality maps for human-alien contact, the official line has gone, is either the Christopher Columbus scenario where earthling space voyagers go where man has never gone before to seek out . . . well, you already know the rest of that riff. The second reality map is the *Close Encounters of the Third Kind* or *Independence Day* scenario where a giant chandelier from Tau Ceti descends to the accompaniment of the celestial music of the spheres and emissaries from the galactic core disembark to either save our skins or blow us to smithereens.

A third reality map, and one that has never been given serious consideration by any publicly declared official sources (other than a mere couple of million ordinary human beings) is a scenario where the aliens have been here for a long time, maybe since neolithic times, and have interacted with and exploited humans since day one for purposes entirely their own.

But it's precisely this scenario that appears, in the

face of anecdotal evidence, to make for a reasonably valid hypothesis—if you want to go looking for one. Moreover, it is this hypothesis that the establishment has never attached much credibility to since the modern UFO debate began at the end of the Second World War.

No matter what the truth may turn out to be, the sheer weight of anecdotal evidence could certainly argue that the facts about alien-human contact run deeper than we have been given to believe by those entrusted with serving the public trust. From the earliest days of the modern awareness of UFO phenomena to the present, hundreds and indeed thousands of witnesses have reported sightings of, and encounters with, other-earthly phenomena that bespeak of alien presences on the planet.

Indeed, these reports antedated the alleged saucer crashes in New Mexico and can be traced back to the final decades of the nineteenth century. They continued during the period of the two world wars—in fact during World War II the USAF received numerous reports from servicemen concerning UFO activity near and over the scenes of major battles. The GIs of World War II called these UFO phenomena "Foo Fighters."

The sightings weren't by any means only confined to the Allied side—the Germans and the Soviets reported them as well. In fact, there are reports that a UFO crash in the region of Spitsbergen, Norway (a group of islands just below the Arctic Circle also known as Svalbard), near the close of the war provided the Nazis with the same opportunity to exploit alien technology that the Roswell crash had supposedly given the United States a few years later (though these "reports" have many of the trappings of rumor, at least to me).

According to the story, Nazi scientists transitioned the most accessible parts of the technology into the crop of superweapons that Hitler boasted would win the war. Whether Hitler's threat was credible or not, the arsenal of the Third Reich boasted sophisticated medium-range ballistic missiles, cruise missiles, jet aircraft, manned rocket aircraft and various other technologies that the Allied side did not then possess, although the research and development efforts of both sides stemmed from a common technology base.[1]

UFO sightings, joined with growing abduction reports and stories of cattle mutilation, continued in the years immediately following the war's end, but these were quickly debunked and the informants subjected to ridicule.

A generation that had come of age during the regimented years of World War II, and which questioned authority far less than succeeding generations, was easily silenced. The ostensible New Mexico saucer crashes seem to mark a watershed or turning point in the clandestine story of the cover-up, a point where a concerted effort to suppress a truth fueled by the terror of coming face to face with the unbelievable led to an organized campaign of silence.

---

1. It should be added that the U.S. and Britain had a sizeable edge over the Germans in critical radar and sonar technologies by the close of the war.

Conspiracy theorists hold that it was President Harry Truman who acquiesced to elements of the then–newly formed National Security Council (NSC) into creating an ultrasecret function under the code name of Majority to deal with the problem.

Majority was controlled by a twelve-member group known as MJ-12 whose members served for life and were replaced only when they died, according to UFOlogists. Majority, which was given supreme executive powers and made nominally responsible only to the president, was tasked with oversight of every aspect of dealing with the new alien reality. It served as an umbrella under which numerous other programs, such as Sigma, Plato, Aquarius and Pounce were created to engage and counter specific aspects of the events.

Among the responsibilities of these programs were human-alien diplomacy, the acquisition of crashed extraterrestrial spacecraft, the testing and reverse-engineering of alien technology and the suppression of the actual reality by means of disinformation, intimidation and, when situations called for it, murder.

There is a certain gut-feel about the credibility of these assertions that sets in when considering some biographical and historical facts concerning President Truman. In his six-volume *History of World War II,* British Prime Minister Winston Churchill displayed a barely concealed dislike, even contempt, for the president who succeeded Franklin Roosevelt, for whom Churchill evidently had a great deal of respect and genuine affection.

Evidently Roosevelt himself shared these feelings for the former senator from Missouri who became his vice president in a bid to garner rural votes, since he confided virtually nothing concerning national policy to Truman, and rarely met with him face to face during the entire term of his unique ten-year presidency. In fact, on Roosevelt's sudden death, Truman knew nothing whatever of some of the most important military plans of the war's end, including the existence of the atomic bomb.

From all appearances Harry Truman was a country boy from a rural constituency who was far out of his depth in most matters concerning the office of the president that he'd just assumed. Truman showed two early traits that earned Churchill's dislike—a willingness to defer to the more authoritarian and hawkish elements in his administration and a naivete concerning the consequences of the use of power. One good example of this is the way Truman handled U.S. nuclear policy.

At the Potsdam conference, where the Allies drew up plans to conclude the war, Truman, newly installed as president, had his first encounter with Soviet Premier Joseph Stalin.

Truman's impression of Stalin, as recorded by Churchill, was of a likeable country bumpkin who wasn't very bright and who he could put in his pocket. Evidently Truman believed that the premier's affability and prodigious consumption of vodka was proof that Stalin was anything but one of the shrewdest and most ruthless political operators since Genghis Khan.

It was in this belief that Truman revealed to Stalin

that America now had something called an atomic bomb, which was very powerful, but otherwise was no big deal, so don't worry about it, Ivan. In his memoirs, Churchill relates with the understated condemnation of the British how Truman slapped his thigh and boasted of having "put one over on Uncle Joe."

In truth, "Uncle Joe" had put one over on Truman. Not only did the Soviets know all about the Manhattan Project, which gave America its fledgling nuclear weapons capability, but his extremely able network of atomic spies had already given the Soviets enough data to start their own nuclear program, one that would soon overtake that of the United States.

Less pardonable was Truman's decision to actually drop the A-bomb on Japan. There's no question that the Nipponese military forces deserved to be shown no mercy. They had attacked Pearl Harbor, conducted the infamous Bataan Death March and been responsible for numerous acts of barbarism and genocide during the war. The use of any weapons, including nuclear, against them would have been completely justified.

There is also no question that to war planners weary and numbed by the most devastating and savage war in the planet's history, the bombing of civilian populations in an effort to shorten the war would have appeared defensible. Members of my own family dropped a few of those bombs on places like Berlin and Dresden in those days, and I can live with that too. War, as they say, is hell, after all.

As Truman himself put it in a letter to the Federal Council of Churches by way of justification for the

A-bombings, "I was greatly disturbed over the unwarranted attack by the Japanese on Pearl Harbor and for their murder of our prisoners of war. The only language they seem to understand is the one we have been using to bombard them. When you have to deal with a beast you have to treat him as a beast."

But the decision to use nuclear weapons against Japan was of a different order of magnitude than other massive bombing attacks of the war. It involved the certain knowledge that hundreds of thousands would die in agony and that most of these would not be combat troops but civilians. Truman had been informed of these numbers beforehand, but he had been told by military advisors that the use of the A-bomb would compensate for those deaths by saving the lives of up to a million U.S. soldiers who would not have to fight a prolonged battle to take the Japanese home islands, one that might add another year to the war.

But these figures are misleading. By this time America had long-range B-29 bombers based on captured islands and atolls that enabled us to reach the Japanese mainland and bomb it with impunity. It's likely that conventional explosives alone might have worked just as well as a nuclear strike. Apart from this, Japan was already beaten and its leaders knew it. In fact the Japanese had been trying to surrender for at least a year prior to the nuclear bombings. However, the Allies insisted on unconditional surrender without offering a precise definition of the term, except that the emperor would have to step down. To the Japanese the abdication of their revered Hirohito would have been unthinkable, and it's unlikely that this was not known by military intelligence. In the end, Hirohito did not have to abdicate, but only after Hiroshima and Nagasaki had been nuked to radioactive rubble.

There were highly placed figures, even then, who shuddered at going nuclear. Churchill—who had never shown the slightest hesitation in using whatever military means possible to win—was one of them, but his pleas to hold off on microwaving Hiroshima were ignored. Churchill surmised in his memoirs that had FDR survived in office to confront the question of using nukes, the outcome might have been considerably different. Eisenhower, also no bleeding heart, on learning of the bombing, was reported to have said, "The Japanese were ready to surrender and it wasn't necessary to hit them with that awful thing." Other staunch supporters of the Allied cause held similar views.

Considering the lack of military justification, the explanation that the bombings were sanctioned as a payback for the Japanese attack on Pearl Harbor and as a demonstration to the Soviets of the awesome weaponry at America's disposal, may come closer to the truth. Another factor may simply have been an inexorable momentum toward testing a revolutionary new weapon that had been developed at incredible cost before the war's end, something not as unthinkable in the blood-soaked summer of 1945 after war had claimed millions upon millions of lives around the world as it appears today.

Nevertheless, Truman's decision was at odds with the views of many of the national leaders on the Allied side, including, as already mentioned, that of Churchill and (posthumously) FDR. The plan to use nuclear weapons on Japan was largely a drive by a group of advocates in intelligence and military circles with isolationist leanings and who had been exerting pressure on FDR to pull out of Europe early in the fighting.

While Roosevelt opposed this view and personally managed the course of the war, Truman's policy was largely hands off. Truman was a president who abrogated decision-making responsibility to other people, much like Ronald Reagan did in a later presidency. He showed this propensity in concessions to the generals and the intelligence chiefs, and it's possible that if Truman was advised to create an organization like Majority he might have done so in the same knee-jerk fashion he did many other things.

If true—and I take no personal stand on whether or not this actually took place—then by doing so Truman would have set in motion a legacy more far-reaching than even the Hiroshima bomb, one that then would deservedly have been dubbed "Cosmic Watergate." Once a cover-up of such magnitude was put in place it would have become impossible to stop, especially in the face of an escalating cold war between the West and a Soviet Bloc that, to some, showed evidence of also having gotten its hands on alien technologies that were transitioned to serve military ends.

When the Eisenhower administration began with a pledge to the American public to "clean up the mess in Washington" left over from the Truman presidency, it could already have been too late to clean up perhaps the biggest Truman mess of all.

By this time, conspiracy theorists assert, Majority had burgeoned to include a secret pact between the U.S. government and alien emissaries that provided humans with esoteric technologies, including spacecraft, in return for noninterference with alien abductions of earthlings for genetic experimentation and for food sources. Some theorize that JFK was assassinated in part because of his plans to end the cover-up and make public the existence of Majority; plans that a powerful "shadow government" that had become entrenched since the Truman administration had no intention of letting happen.

Yet, cover-up or no cover-up, the reports of sightings and abductions not only didn't abate but actually increased. The abduction phenomenon has always been the least believable and of a kind most likely to garner ridicule for self-proclaimed abductees, but it has nevertheless refused to die down. Not only has it persisted but has been reported in all parts of the world and from members of all cultures, ethnic groups and political systems.

Most abductees have never shown any prior history of psychosis, distorted reality perception or delusional mental states or other mental pathology, and their accounts share common details that repeat themselves over and over. Among these details are those not generally known to the public at large.

While many of these details only come out under hypnosis, there is sizeable portion (about 20 percent) who can recall what happened spontaneously. Also to be considered is that liars and crazy people would not be expected to spin tales as complicated or as cohesive as the reports of abductees, and then have them all agree in such great numbers across several decades of report gathering. Clearly, something strange seems to be happening.

The most commonly reported alien type is what has become familiar to us as the "Grey," a being of between three to five feet in height, with a large, praying mantis–like head dominated by two huge, black, opaque teardrop-shaped eyes with vertically slit pupils, a small mouth and absent or atrophied ears and nose. It is believed that Greys have atrophied digestive systems and absorb nutrients through their skins, mixed with chemical agents such as hydrogen peroxide.

Nevertheless it is claimed that humans and Greys are genetically related; some claims go so far as to state that humans were created by Greys in past millennia. There are said to be several species of Greys with slightly varying physical characteristics and levels of hostility to humankind.

Another commonly reported alien is known as the "Nordic" type. Again, there are several different flavors of alien here too, but they are predominantly characterized as being of giant stature with blond hair and other stereotypically Nordic features. Obviously, the Nordics are a humanoid type that would be even more closely related to earthlings than the Greys. Nevertheless, the Nordics are considered as hostile to terrans as the diminutive Greys, and in any case have been said to follow a policy of complete noninterference with the plight of human abductees.

A third common alien type is known as Reptilians or Reptoids. They resemble the Greys but are physically larger and more robust. They have less of the insect genetic strain in their makeup and more of the saurian. Indeed, they most closely resemble what one of the smaller species of dinosaurs might look like if it had evolved to the point where it lost its tail, walked upright and wore street clothes. Of the three alien types, the Reptoids are considered by alien theorists as the most hostile to humankind.

Abductions are said to last for about two hours, though many have involved shorter intervals and not all have taken place aboard alien craft. The procedures conducted on abductees supposedly involve the implantation of various biological tracking and control devices inserted into or near the brain through nasal or ear cavities and the programming of abductees to perform posthypnotic activities.

Another common procedure is the impregnation of, and ova extraction from, human females and extraction of sperm from human males for the purposes of various sophisticated genetic procedures that include the crossbreeding of human-alien hybrids and the production of biological android or synthetic entities. In some cases, however, abductees are said to have been used for purposes of food and as sources of sadistic pleasure by their alien captors.

In many instances, aliens have imparted religious or quasi-religious explanations to abductees to justify their actions. These explanations usually are reported to take the form of divine right to experiment on humans in furtherance of some greater cosmic end in the mutual interest of both human and alien species—a sort of "Trust me, I'm an alien" manipulation gambit.

Likewise, professed abductees commonly report that the aliens justify their clandestine methods of operating on and mind-control manipulation of their victims by claims that on the one hand physically larger and stronger humans could pose a threat to them if angered and, on the other, that their super brains give off emanations that could prove harmful to puny earthlings. If nothing else, this proves that talking out of both sides of the mouth is a truly universal practice.

Sometimes alien procedures and exposure hazards result in the alleged deaths of humans. Other times abductees are healed or cured by these same weird energies. Often humans are told nothing, but at other times they are given all sorts of information and in some cases even encouraged to go forth and preach a new gospel of cosmic oneness provided by their alien mentors.

But the database of sightings and abduction reports is full of anomalies of all kinds, despite its many points of agreement. In fact, there is an entire class of abductees who repeat, over and over, with the same striking regularity evidenced in the bulk of reports, that not Greys or Nordics or even Reptoids have kidnapped them, but beings out of ancient myth such as Horus, the Egyptian falcon-headed god of birth, death and fertility.

By the same token, there is a well-documented category of UFO sightings classed as the "living organism" type that resemble amoebic or viral forms and a large number of reports where the objects changed shape and size while being viewed. These documentable reports contradict those equally significant reports of solid or hard objects and humanoid aliens in corporeal bodies. There are also the so-called "mothman" sightings of winged, headless beings with a heavy thirst for blood—bovine or human.

In this class of sightings are stories concerning the so-called "men in black." These are not two funny dudes in Silva Thin shades who go around whacking bad aliens and zapping earthling memories with "the flashy thing" such as in the Spielberg movie of the same name, but weird, not-quite-humans who have been reported to do scary things to persons who've encountered them. They do share sartorial preferences with Tommy Lee Jones and Will Smith, though; the MIB are reported to dress all in black, showing a penchant for black turtlenecks and black ball caps—and yes—real dark shades too.

The MIB also are said to share Messrs. Smith and Jones's preference for wheels, as they are reported to drive around in big, black car service–style limos. But the MIB don't just drive, they also fly—in mysterious black helicopters that have been reported to actively harass victims. In most reported cases, avowed contactees describe encounters with MIB after trespassing on government property or after abductions by aliens.

It's conjectured by some that MIB are androids or other clonal entities created by Majority in emulation of alien procedures and used as enforcement personnel to protect the government's stake in the Cosmic Watergate coverup and to gather genetic material for Majority-sanctioned projects, often by way of human-sponsored cattle mutilations.

Some theorists have coined the phrase "Trojan Horse effect" to explain the contradictions in the database of UFO phenomena. The effect takes its name from the deception that gave rise to the famous Latin phrase *timeo Danaos et dona ferentes* or "beware of Greeks bearing gifts." UFOlogists have coined still another phrase, "the Great Deception," to explain the historic picture of the way in which aliens have interacted with humans.

In this reality map, the aliens have revealed themselves to us in ways consonant with the human thinking of any given era. In Biblical times, it was as manifestations of the Divine Presence on earth; in later times it was as miraculous mass epiphanies such as the Fatima revelation of 1910. In more current times, where the scientific and rationalist model has held sway, they have assumed the form of spacecraft and extraterrestrials.

In all cases, proponents of the Great Deception theory point out that some as yet unexplainable phenomena beyond human understanding has manifested itself in these varying forms and that the cosmic cover-up has been going on, in various guises, since the dawn of civilization itself.

This observer's gut feel is that both the "hard" model and the "soft" model are both pertinent and that one may be as "real" as the other—if either is real at all, that is. A parallel might be seen in the way light was regarded by scientists when it was first studied. Light was first thought to be corpuscular, that is, it seemed made up of discrete particles of energy that were transmitted in pulses called photons.

The particle or photonic theory can be measured— you can even see actual photons of light in a pitch-dark room if you look hard enough. So photons exist. But by the same token light is also wavelike and these waves, which cannot be divided into particles like photons, also unquestionably exist. So what is light? Is it photons or is it waves? Only with the emergence of modern quantum theory was the matter resolved—light is both or either, depending on the observer's frame of reference.

So what are aliens? To me the answer is perfectly clear—if they actually exist, they're welcome to leave, and good riddance.

IMPACT ANALYSIS

The possibility of a cover-up of human-alien contact by government agencies would represent the biggest can of worms ever presented to the human race if proven to exist. Small wonder that if there was actually a conspiracy to hide the truth, it would go to extreme lengths to keep the truth hidden. Nevertheless, in the face of stories of abductions, livestock mutilations and even human deaths related to UFO phenomena, the existence of a cover-up is more than just academic, but is a real-world issue that needs to be better explained by officialdom than it currently is.

XII ⚏

Sex and Death in the White House

As these words are written, Bill Clinton has gone on TV to tell the nation that he didn't exactly give us the whole truth about his affair with Monica Lewinsky. Like I'm sure was the case with millions of other viewers, I was completely surprised by this revelation. Bowled over. Flabbergasted. Discombobulated. Flummoxed. Crazed. I sat there in such a state of shock that it was literally hours before I came to my senses again, shouting things like, "What a revelation! Amazing! Holy Stromboli!"

I mean, why in the world would I doubt Clinton's word when he said he never had an affair with the astonishingly beautiful, charmingly poised and stunningly shaped 21-year-old White House intern? Just because similar accusations of hanky-panky had been made by a circus tent full of people since he was governor of Arkansas? No way! Just because I personally have a prodigious, if bent, intellect and a "hands problem" when I'm around women? Of course not. Never!

Bill denied those ridiculous charges of fooling around with dozens of ladies who practically threw themselves at him again and again, so naturally it had to be true. I mean, the president was telling us this, for crissakes! Furthermore, when Bill had an astonishingly beautiful, charmingly poised and stunningly shaped wife like Hillary, why on earth would Bill have any reason to even cast a single lustful glance at any other woman? Obviously, this reason alone lent the strongest credibility to our fearless leader's denials.

So you can be sure old Dave was totally dumbfounded when the prez said he'd varnished the truth some to cover up that he was getting a little more than just paperwork from a young girl who served under him. And don't think Dave's just being sarcastic here. Never, I tell you—never would I ever use sarcasm about such a serious matter! I really mean this. Honest. I was shocked—shocked to the very core! Shocked, I tell you!

But now that I've calmed down a little I can admit to myself that maybe the hanky-panky that's been alleged to have gone on at the Clinton White House isn't that strange after all. In fact, as my blood pressure drops and my crazed howls of disbelief subside, I can accept that, at least by comparison with some of the historical revelations concerning the sex lives of preceding presidents, Bill's peccadillos are pretty tame.

In fact, as my crazed, stunned howls become more like the usual grunts, snide chuckles and four-letter words I spout when sitting down to write, I can admit to myself that no boner that Bill's ever pulled in the hanky-panky department can match those of his hero, the late Jack Kennedy—or one or two other presidents besides, for that matter. After all, as the saying goes, where there's a will, there's a way. And where there's a Bill, there's a—well, you get my drift.

It's never been a secret that JFK was a womanizer who cheated on the missus every chance he got. What hasn't come out, until recently, has been the almost unbelievable recklessness of Kennedy's presidential screwing around, a recklessness that could very likely have cost him his presidency had Kennedy not been assassinated in Dallas, Texas, on November 22, 1963.

In the book *The Dark Side of Camelot,* journalist Seymour Hersh presents highly credible accounts from eyewitnesses concerning JFK's sexual escapades while occupying the White House as president of the United States. Other eyewitness accounts were also given on the ABC News special *Dangerous World: The Kennedy Years,* which aired twice in the spring and summer of 1998.

According to the accounts, JFK's brother Bobby, serving as U.S. Attorney General, shared in many of these pornographic frolics, including regular nude romps in a hot tub with a bevy of Capitol Hill bimbos.

The credibility of the many new revelations is bolstered by the fact that these bombshells are only the latest in a series of JFK biographies and memoirs of those connected with the late president, such as Judith Campbell, a self-avowed Kennedy mistress.

How much is forgivable depends on your personal moral barometer. Being no saint, I can personally turn a blind eye to some of Kennedy's partying, or at least accept it in theory. What I can't forgive are those allegations that JFK gratified his own fleshly hankerings at the expense of the safety of the nation he was sworn to protect. In those instances, he may have placed the lives of millions of other Americans on the line and increased the risk of nuclear war between the United States and the Soviet Union.

In JFK's case, the sheer quantity of his encounters was a factor that could have put his life in jeopardy. Secret Service agents are said to have been shocked at the lack of precautions Kennedy took. They were under orders to admit women to the president without even a search of their handbags. Apart from the possibility that any of those women could have been KGB agents carrying a syringe filled with poison, or a spy camera with which to film compromising photos, or any number of other dangerous items, it's almost certain that some of them were reporting back to the intelligence agencies of other countries, including the Soviet Union.

There is no reason to assume that the Soviet political elite was ever as puritanical as they made out, but by the same token there is no reason to believe that then–Soviet Premier Nikita Khrushchev would see Ken-

nedy's escapades as anything but further proof of
JFK's lack of moral fiber.[1] By this time Khrushchev—
who was a protégé of hard-liner Joseph Stalin, a man
who reputedly prized vodka above sex any day of the
week—had already formed a negative opinion of Kennedy in this regard, and in the Soviet mind this was
directly associated with a leader's will and decision-
making acumen.

Intelligence reports of Kennedy's orgies—to say
nothing of his recurring speed injections from the president's Dr. Feelgood, Max Jacobsen—reaching Khrushchev's ears could certainly have further lowered his
estimate of the U.S. president and led him to believe
that he might get away with shipping nuclear missiles
to Cuba under our noses, precipitating the Cuban missile crisis that almost led to nuclear war. Of course,
JFK's single-minded, even obsessive, efforts to undermine Castro and oust the communists from Cuba
(which continued even after the missile crisis was resolved), including the ill-fated Bay of Pigs invasion,
was a precipitating factor in the Soviet deployment of
nukes to Cuba.

---

1. Dissident Yugoslavian communist Milovan Djilas wrote the following in *Conversations with Stalin* (Penguin, 1967) concerning a
Soviet state banquet he attended during the heyday of the Stalin era:
"Girls who were too pretty and too extravagantly made up to be
waitresses brought in vast quantities of the choicest victuals . . . Even
earlier one could see that the Soviet officers were secretly looking
forward to the feast." Djilas later on relates an attempt by Soviet
intelligence to set him up with a Moscow prostitute. The book also
describes Stalin's penchant for telling crude jokes and his repeated
challenging of his dinner guests to no-holds-barred drinking bouts.

Kennedy's affair with a Washington, D.C., "party girl" named Ellen Rometsch, who was possibly also a spy for the East German intelligence service, STASI (also known as the SDD), and therefore the Soviet KGB, confirms that other presidential sex partners could have been spies as well. In the case of Rometsch, once her alleged past communist affiliations were discovered and their implications to the presidency perceived, she was paid off to quickly leave the country.

The Profumo scandal, in which the British war minister, John Profumo, was brought down by his affair with call girl Christine Keeler, was fresh in the public mind and was a wake-up call to those close to JFK, including his brother Bobby. Like Rometsch, Keeler had connections to Soviet intelligence by way of a Russian case officer stationed in London with whom Keeler was closely linked. Bobby Kennedy is said to have handled the arrangements to spirit Rometsch out of the country, as he'd fixed other problems for his elder brother.

Though Rometsch was safely out of the country during the final weeks of JFK's life, reports of her liaison with Kennedy were already filtering into the media and had been taken up as the possible subject of a probe by members of Congress, who were talking of plans to return Rometsch to the United States to testify in an investigation of Kennedy's extracurricular White House activities.

Had Kennedy lived past that fateful November day in Dallas, it is highly likely that these developments would have led to an American version of the Profumo scandal involving both Kennedy brothers in the White House. It would likely have either ended in the ouster of the president or his loss of the next presidential election. In this light, regardless of whether or not Kennedy had been stopped by a bullet or his own philandering, it's tempting to conjecture about the extent to which history would have actually been changed in the long run.

Another dangerous liaison between JFK and a woman was the affair he had with Judith Campbell, who was also the girlfriend of Chicago Mafia boss Sam Giancana. It's alleged that Campbell acted as a link between the Kennedy White House and the Chicago wise guys as well as a courier for cash and other forms of payola between the White House, La Cosa Nostra and elements of what had been coined the "military industrial complex" by White House think-tanker Robert McNamara.

Kennedy might even possibly be excused concerning his dealings with the Mafia because, after all, the Mafia had been a covert partner in U.S. intelligence operations since the invasion of Sicily in World War II. At that time the "Honorable Society" was the only source of post-fascist stability and order in the south of Italy, apart from the communists, which U.S. military intelligence wanted no dealings with whatsoever.

Roosevelt, Truman and Eisenhower before Kennedy had all, directly or indirectly, done the occasional deal with the Italian Mafia as a wartime legacy of organized crime's participation in government initiatives. In JFK's case, however, added familiarity might well have bred added contempt and ultimately become a factor in the plot to assassinate him.[2]

Interestingly enough, JFK's successor to the presidency, Lyndon Baines Johnson, rivaled Kennedy's escapades, even though Johnson was far uglier than his former boss, so homely in fact that a popular '60s slogan button read, "No More Ugly Children—Sterilize LBJ!"

Homely or not, Johnson's presidential philandering was in terms of sheer quantity in the same league as Kennedy's, and Johnson apparently made no secret of it. In fact, LBJ is reputed to have enjoyed boasting of his performance with his sex partners every chance he got, and White House staff had to listen to the commander in chief's crude, play-by-play descriptions on a regular basis. Unlike today, the media of the era dutifully covered everything up, as it had done with Kennedy and previous presidents.

Some feminists have characterized Bill Clinton as a "sexual predator" in the wake of the Jones and Lewinsky allegations, but Bill's got nothing on Lyndon in that department if a famous story about LBJ can be believed. Here, a young female White House intern

---

2. My coverage of this subject is limited by space. For more on the JFK–organized crime connection there are numerous sources, including *Blood and Power* (Penguin, 1989).

was staying overnight at the Johnson ranch in Texas. In the middle of the night she awakened to find a man in a nightshirt standing by her bed holding a flashlight. She couldn't recognize her guest's face in the darkness of the room, but she recognized the telltale LBJ drawl when her visitor intoned, "Move ovah, this is yore presidunt!"

In 1987, a thirty-six-year-old man claiming to be Johnson's illegitimate son and sole living heir, filed a $10.5 million patrimony suit against the Johnson estate. Steven Brown claimed that his mother, sixty-two-year-old Madeleine Brown, had been Johnson's mistress for some twenty-one years.

Madeleine herself claimed that LBJ set her up with a house, a maid, charge cards with unlimited credit and a new car every two years, among other perks. She produced a letter from Johnson's attorney shortly after LBJ's death promising to keep up the arrangements now that he'd gone to that big cattle ranch in the sky.

LBJ had an even longer fling going with a woman named Alice Glass, according to Robert A. Caro's LBJ biography, published in 1982. The Caro biography gave compelling evidence of a thirty-year affair between Johnson and Glass. In this case, Glass also happened to be the girlfriend of Virginia newspaper publisher Charles E. Marsh, who was Johnson's mentor at the time he met Glass. In the event, LBJ had the best of both worlds, help from a powerful meister at a critical time in his career and some down-home southern comfort from Marsh's girlfriend.

If the end of the thirty-year affair, which allegedly

came in 1967, proves anything, it's that there's never an ill wind that blows somebody some good—Glass supposedly ditched LBJ for good because he was making war, not love, in Vietnam. Seems her social conscience couldn't handle that rumble in the Southeast Asian jungle, and there was no contact between them after that. If so, then it was surely good news for Lady Bird, Johnson's wife—were it not for 'Nam, she probably would never have seen her marriage partner anymore.

🧩 In some ways stranger even than JFK's or LBJ's White House whoopie-making was that of Franklin Delano Roosevelt.

FDR and his wife, Eleanor, had ceased having marital relations early on in their marriage. In 1918, while FDR was serving as assistant secretary of the navy, Eleanor found a bunch of love letters addressed to her husband from another woman.

The fact that it was Eleanor's own social secretary, Lucy Page Mercer, who'd written the letters, was an even unkinder cut. Since a divorce—which the devastated Eleanor favored—was tantamount to political suicide, FDR nixed it. Franklin agreed to drop Lucy, but his marriage to Eleanor became a political partnership arrangement after that. At the White House, the two slept in separate bedrooms and led entirely separate lives.

By all accounts, this open marriage was open in every sense of the word. In contrast to the carryings-on of other White House administrations, FDR's menage with his personal secretary, Missy LeHand, was totally out in front. Eleanor knew about it and accepted it. Elliot Roosevelt, son of Franklin and Eleanor, has written that it was not uncommon to find Missy draped in a nightgown in FDR's White House bedroom early in the morning.

Eleanor had her own clique of buddies, most of them women, especially Nancy Cook, New York Democratic Party head of the women's division and Marion Dickerman, headmistress of a private school where Eleanor taught part-time. Cook, who wore her hair close-cropped and was usually seen chomping on a stogie, and schoolmarm Dickerman moved in with Eleanor at her upstate New York estate, Val-Kill.

But it was Eleanor's special girlfriend, "Hick," who played the most important role in her life. Lorena Hickok, was an Associated Press reporter working the political beat who was reputedly a lesbian.

While there was never an open admission that Hick and Eleanor shared a lesbian relationship, there are eighteen cardboard boxes full of letters that the two women exchanged that argue somewhat differently. In the letters, one aches to hold the other close, another recalls the tender touch of mouth against lips, and more kissy-kissy, mushy-mushy stuff of a similar nature.

Hick moved into the Roosevelt White House in 1941 and stayed for the next four years, and she and the first lady were reportedly as close as two peas in a pod. At the same time, it was not uncommon to find Missy sitting on FDR's lap in the Oval Office or bedecked in one of her nightgowns in the president's private suite, as already mentioned.

And these are just the highlights. There's more, not just about FDR and LBJ, that I haven't gotten to and about most other presidents too—lack of space and a desire to eat my lunch without hurling demands that I put these ruminations to a close right now. But suffice it to say that Eisenhower, Woodrow Wilson, even Thomas Jefferson and George Washington (you think he's called "the father of our country" for nothing?) were all doing the hanky-panky while serving as president of the United States.

And yes, folks, there was even a woman in Richard Milhous Nixon's life who some have alleged he spent time with behind his wife's back. No spit! Her name was Marianna Liu, a cocktail hostess at the Hong Kong Hilton, who Nixon is said to have met on one of his numerous visits to the Orient in the mid-sixties. You can bet your Spiro that Nixon's trip to the Great Wall in 1970 wasn't the only overture to the Chinese that he made in his time, and that's one thing that's perfectly clear.

If all this proves anything, it's that any zipper problem Bill's got ain't much compared to that of his predecessors. So let's all lighten up on the dude, okay? Besides, which do you think is the worse lie—Bill's "I never had an affair with Monica Lewinsky" or George Bush's "Read my lips—NO NEW TAXES!"

I rest my case.

■► Another scandal that rocked the Clinton White House involved the death by suicide of presidential legal counsel Vincent Foster. Soon after Foster's demise was made public, conspiracy theories began to sprout faster than tadpoles in a pond full of slime and gave rise to what quickly became known as "Fostergate."

Foster's death marked only the second suicide by a member of the White House staff in U.S. history. The first and only other such demise was that of Secretary of the Navy James V. Forrestal, a White House staff member during the Truman administration. Another similarity that Forrestal's demise shared with Foster's is that it too didn't take place on White House grounds.

In 1949, Forrestal took his life by jumping from a sixteenth-story window. The window in question happened to be in his room at Bethesda Naval Hospital in Washington, D.C., where Forrestal was being treated for what was termed "advanced paranoid schizophrenia."

Forrestal had developed these symptoms after the end of the Second World War, as Soviet troops overran Eastern Europe. Just before killing himself, Forrestal was heard screaming that Jews and communists were crawling around the floor of his room, seeking to destroy him.

Like Foster's death, Forrestal's demise quickly gave rise to numerous conspiracy theories. These have grown instead of diminished with the passage of time. Forrestal was supposed to have been one of the original members of MJ-12, the ultrasecret, presidentially appointed working group designated to investigate and cover up human-alien encounters and UFO sightings and landings that was allegedly established by Harry S. Truman.

One version of the conspiracy theory has it that his "suicide" was staged by the CIA because Forrestal had threatened to expose the presence of superintelligent praying mantises from another solar system on earth in the wake of the Roswell crash two years before his window-diving stunt.

However there's another explanation, the simple and obvious one that Forrestal had in fact totally lost his marbles. Long before his being committed to a mental institution, Forrestal was at the center of right-wing, paranoid conspiracies to help the Nazis gain power.

In 1938, Forrestal was sitting on the board of I. G. Chemie, the U.S. subsidiary of the infamous German firm, I. G. Farben, which in turn was part of an operation to run Nazi intelligence agents in the United States, among other things. After the war, Forrestal was one of those instrumental in making sure that Germany's Nazi-owned industrial base remained virtually intact.

With his heroes Hitler, Himmler, Goering and other Nazi "supermen" gone to rat Valhalla, it's not surprising that Forrestal slipped his cogs. To his kind, a world without the sound of jackboots and hoarse-throated *Sieg-Heil*s probably wasn't a place conducive to sanity.

🧩 But—back to Foster, whose more recent death also sparked a swirl of conspiracy theories to explain what was in all likelihood the suicide of a profoundly depressed Little Rock lawyer who in Washington,

D.C., found himself caught in a world he'd never made. Back home in Arkansas, Foster had been part of a triumvirate at the prestigious Rose Law Firm that included Hillary Clinton and Webster Hubbell, who also became part of the Clinton White House team.

Hillary, Vince and Hubbell together made up the Rose firm's litigation unit, handling the noncorporate cases that were new to Rose's practice. Foster was especially close to Hillary at Rose, as frequently found with her at Rose board meetings as at social settings outside the firm; however, there is little reason to think that they were ever more than "just good friends," as the saying goes, despite claims to the contrary.

Then, with the transition to the White House, Foster found himself embroiled in the mounting legal problems that quickly began to confront and overwhelm the Clintons. Among these was the complex of issues that collectively became known as "Whitewater," which involved not only the Clintons' investment in the failed Whitewater land development project but also included Hillary's profits from livestock futures investments through a well-placed friend, James Blair, and also connections to the Madison Guaranty Savings and Loan collapse, a bank run by Whitewater developer James McDougal.

It had been McDougal who had persuaded the Clintons to invest in Whitewater in the first place. McDougal had been Bill Clinton's political mentor in Arkansas and, as a real estate speculator, had specialized in land flips that often generated sizable profits.

Having made a large profit on a small investment in a deal done by McDougal, the Clintons were well dis-

posed to become partners with McDougal in the Whitewater Development Company, which was developing
a tract of land along Arkansas' White River. Considering McDougal's excellent track record in prior real
estate deals, neither the Clintons nor McDougal himself had any reason to doubt that the Whitewater deal
would rake in a handsome profit for all concerned.

Unfortunately, in the end that's not the way things
turned out. Through a series of mishaps, snafus and
bad judgment calls, Whitewater became a tar baby instead of a gold mine. The problems for the Clintons
were compounded when McDougal, in a later incar-
nation as president of the Madison Trust Savings Bank
he'd established in the small town of Kingston, Arkansas, ran afoul of federal banking regulations and faced
charges of fiscal mismanagement.

McDougal's banking practices allegedly violated
federal banking regulations in part by loans he'd made
to himself to pay off the mounting Whitewater debt.
The Clintons' problems were exacerbated by Hillary's
refusal to sell their share of Whitewater back to
McDougal and thereby remove the albatross from
around the Clintons' necks. By the time the Clintons
arrived in Washington, a series of apparently innocent
but incredibly knotty financial boondoggles had snow-
balled into a Gorgon's head of problems with fangs.

Foster saw the Whitewater conflict threaten to engulf
the Clinton presidency as his boss's first term drew to
a close, and he'd also seen Hubbell brought down,
forced to resign from the White House staff by charges
of financial misappropriation from the Rose firm. Put-

ting in grueling hours at the White House, Foster was growing profoundly depressed and toward the end, more erratic in his behavior. A perfunctory file-photo request from the reputedly anti-Clinton *Wall Street Journal,* for example, threw Foster into a panic, as did a few lines about him in a *Wall Street Journal* article, in part precipitated by his refusal to comply with the original photo request.

A paranoid fear of being caught in the net of legal troubles that had enmeshed his friends now gripped Foster in an ever-tightening mental noose. Foster's way out was to use the silver .38-caliber revolver that he had brought to Washington from Little Rock against his wife's wishes, a gun that had been bequeathed to him as part of his late father's firearms collection.

Foster's suicide might seem strange on the surface, but suicidal minds don't necessarily follow rational patterns of cause and effect. Others have taken their own lives for less compelling reasons than Foster's largely unfounded fears and level of perceived emotional stress. This happens all the time, despite the superficial absurdity of such senseless acts.

Nevertheless, conspiracy theories were almost destined to arise in the wake of Foster's untimely demise. Many of these centered on the fact that Foster's death was declared a suicide with seemingly inordinate speed, which in fact is not untrue. Adding to the intrigue was the secrecy involved in making Foster's White House papers available to the police and other investigatory bodies, as well as the chance discovery of the torn fragments of a note in Foster's handwriting that, when pieced together, showed indications that Foster was profoundly troubled and depressed.

The physical circumstances of Foster's apparent suicide were also questioned by conspiracy buffs. Foster's body was found in a section of Fairfax County, Virginia's Fort Marcy Park known to be a meeting place for gays seeking "companionship." Park police who first saw the body described it as lying on its back, as though "ready for the coffin." Foster's revolver was still clutched in his hand, and had no detectable blood on it. There was also a mysterious absence of blood spatters near the body. Experts stated that there should have been "pools of blood" near the corpse. The death scene was described as "strange" and "peculiar" by park police.

But no matter how conspiracy theorists try to embroider the unquestionable weirdness of Foster's demise, there are some obvious explanations for what took place.

The lack of blood can be explained by the fact that the bullet that killed Foster went clean through the back of his head (he'd shot himself in the mouth), and the position of the body. There was in fact a substantial pool of blood soaking the ground where Foster's head had been when the corpse was rolled over, and more blood soaked the back of his shirt.

His body lay on the downslope of a small hill, and blood that would have normally flowed from his wounds instead pooled in his lower extremities. The "ready for the coffin" position of the corpse can be explained by the fact that when Foster shot himself he was sitting on the ground and fell backward with his hands flung out to his sides as the bullet tore through his skull.

One explanation I do have questions about is the assertion that Foster continued to clutch his gun in death because his thumb had become trapped between the trigger and the trigger guard of the suicide weapon. Depending on which thumb we're talking about (the thumb pulling the trigger or the thumb of the second hand presumably stabilizing the gun), the precise definition of "trapped" and the actual way in which the gun was "clutched" in Foster's outflung hand, this might or might not be a supportable scenario. But not having viewed actual crime scene photos of the body, I'm not in a position to do anymore than raise a question mark here.

The credibility of the Foster suicide notwithstanding, the evasiveness with which an embattled White House treated Foster's death contributed to the swarm of conspiracy theories that rapidly sprung up, and the speculation has yet to stop. Among the theories are that Foster was part of a global conspiracy financed by Tyson Foods and Wal-Mart (both Arkansas firms) and tied in to a diverse array of persons, places and things, including convicted spy Jonathan Pollard, George Bush, Caspar Weinberger, the BCCI banking scandal, Iran-Contra and former CIA director William Casey's planned "October Surprise."

Foster—like Forrestal—was said to have been murdered because he was about to go public with the whole enchilada and had to be permanently silenced. Others claim Foster had a secret sex hideaway where he and Hillary got it on, or that Foster was gay and had developed AIDS, or that Foster was a secret bagman for the CIA and other intelligence agencies who made regular money runs to hush-hush Swiss bank accounts, something he'd supposedly begun doing as a gofer for BCCI during the rogue bank's freewheeling heyday. And there are yet more theories besides these.

The one thing I'm sure of here is that though Foster may be dead, the conspiraholic feeding frenzy triggered by his suicide will not only be churning up froth for a long while yet (talk about your "white water"), but will just keep getting stranger and stranger as time goes by.

IMPACT ANALYSIS

Attacks by the ousted party on the incumbent administration are nothing new—potshots at Roman emperors were taken whenever possible by opponents who'd been cast from favor by a new regime. Nor is there anything unheard of about scandal in the White House. What *is* new is the practice of launching coordinated attacks on a sitting president by the political opposition for predominantly political ends. Apart from their costing millions of dollars that might have gone toward nobler ends, the attacks have had a spoiling effect on the president's ability to do his job. Investigations into serious wrongdoing should rightfully be pursued, but political witch hunting supposedly went out with McCarthy.

XIII ✜

Afterword: Memo from the Ministry of Love

Bill Clinton's four-hour videotaped grand jury testimony, which was televised on September 22, 1998, as I was wrapping up the writing of this book, ties in with what I said at the outset: conspiracies and cover-ups have direct, everyday consequences for everybody.

After viewing the tapes, the impression I was left with, above all others, was the Orwellian dialectic of the byplay between the president and his interrogators. If our fearless leader wasn't using words and phrases that could have come straight out of the Newspeak dictionary from the novel *1984*, then I'll eat my master's in American lit.

Make no mistake: the president was speaking as he did for good reason. He had been goofing off on company time and been caught red-handed, and we who put him in office had a right to call him on the carpet for it.

Yet, questions of possible perjury aside, by no stretch of the imagination could Clinton, on the face of the evidence, be deemed remotely guilty of the "high crimes and misdemeanors" necessary to make a credible case for impeachment and this, supposedly, was what the investigation was all about.

After some $40 million of taxpayers' money and some four years spent on the probe, this fact was surely evident to the Starr panel too. The videotapes made it abundantly clear that the prosecutors' true aims were different from those they avowed.

And so Clinton twisted and turned, unable to speak the truth that was in itself not damning by any objective standard, but would have done him serious harm nevertheless, apropos a tribunal of Grand Inquisitors bent on destroying him, feigning purity of purpose but governed by a predetermined secret agenda of partisan bias.

How many times have all of us been in that place, with our jobs and maybe our futures hanging in the balance? Unable to speak our minds, unable to tell them where to get off, because to do so would be to be branded a heretic, or politically incorrect, or not a team player, or having an "attitude problem," or guilty of something akin to what Orwell called "thought-crime."

Yet, here we are. In an increasingly corporatized culture of sanitized facades and corrupt interiors, of deceit-filled groupthink and schizoid evasions, where "yes" as often as not means "no," and where the paranoid fear that "they" will get you if you don't watch out may, in at least some cases, be more than just mere paranoia.

When did we start drifting down this road? Was it when Jack Kennedy stopped that legendary "single bullet" on that fateful November day? Was it when Nixon didn't burn those tapes (or indeed when he sanctioned the cover-up, if not the break-in itself)? Or was it the sum total of many things, large and small, much of which went unnoticed even as it happened?

Conspiracy theorists posit a deliberate, interlocking, overarching master plan to explain these developments, but I have my doubts. It could simply be that there's an historical drift toward a less "free" society, at least by previous definitions of the word "freedom," and that the price for a more peaceful and stable world is the imposition of a corporate-style global technocracy, and that this is the true "new world order" that is in store for us.

If so, it's a drift that's been propelled by the increasing partnership of global business interests with government and a style of management native to commercial enterprises that has transformed the way government runs itself, turning politicians into technocrats and cutting more and more of the bottom line from public works programs of every type.

It's a drift from a government of ideals to a government of balance sheets, a change from a humanistic standard of values to one based on indifferent calculations of advantage and disadvantage, profit and loss, status seeking and the application of leverage.

It's a drift toward a society that enshrines cynicism and disdains compassion, but has so lost its ethical footing that it does not even dare to admit its duplicity to itself and so is forced into the ultimate cover-up— the chronic self-deception of Orwellian doublethink.

In this case, the most dangerous conspiracy of all may well be the conspiracy of silence that nurtures this tragic state of affairs on the part of those who should know better. If we're not careful, it may usher us all into a future many times more bleak, and one, unlike today, from which there is no longer a way back to the place we started.

APPENDIX
Acronyms Found in This Book

1WG: One World Government

ACTD: advanced concept technology demonstration

BCCI: Bank of Credit and Commerce International

BND: German intelligence service

BWC: Biological Weapon Convention

CBW: chemical-biological weapons

CFR: Council on Foreign Relations

CIA: Central Intelligence Agency

CONUS: Continental United States

CWC: Chemical Weapon Convention

DARPA: Defense Advanced Research Projects Agency

DIA: Defense Intelligence Agency

DOD: Department of Defense

EBE: extraterrestrial biological entity

ELF: extra low frequency

EMP: electromagnetic pulse

FEMA: Federal Emergency Management Agency

FSU: former Soviet Union

Appendix

G-5: U.S. Seventh Army military intelligence in WWII

GAO: General Accounting Office

GRU: Soviet military intelligence

HAARP: High Frequency Active Auroral Research Project

KE: kinetic energy rounds

LSD: Lysergic Acid Diethylamide-25

MIB: men in black

MOPP: mission oriented protective posture

NORAD: North American Aerospace Defense Command

NSA: National Security Agency

NSC: National Security Council

NWO: New World Order

ODESSA: brotherhood of ex–SS officers

ONI: Office of Naval Intelligence

OOO: *Okhrana Osobykh Ob'ektov* ("Triple-Os")

OSS: Office of Strategic Services

OUVGOSG: Russian Directorate for the Protection of Important State Objectives and Special Cargoes

PLYWD: precision low-yield weapons design

PX: Philadelphia Experiment

RAF: British Royal Air Force

R&D: research and development

Appendix

RHIC: radio-hypnotic intracerebral memory technology

SDD: former East German intelligence agency also known as Stasi

SDECE: former French intelligence service (pronounced Seh-deek)

SDI: Strategic Defense Initiative

SS: *Shutzstaffel*; elite Nazi brigades under Himmler

STRATCOM: Strategic Air Command

TLC: Trilateral Commission

USAF: United States Air Force

USN: United States Navy